OCME

Life in America's Top Forensic Medical Center

BRUCE GOLDFARB

STEERFORTH PRESS
LEBANON, NEW HAMPSHIRE

For information about permission to reproduce
selections from this book, write to:
Steerforth Press L.L.C., 31 Hanover Street, Suite 1
Lebanon, New Hampshire 03766

Cataloging-in-Publication Data is available from the Library of Congress

ISBN 978-1-58642-358-2

Printed in the United States of America

For George and Helane, Jonathan Maxell, and Phillip

CONTENTS

CHAPTER ONE

ONCE IN A LIFETIME

September 10, 2014

Hunched over by the front door of my office building, trying to find the shade, I squint at my phone to read a text from my wife about picking me up after work. My garish red Hawaiian shirt and old-school canvas sneakers add a colorful splash to the West Baltimore corner as I stand next to the gleaming blue windows of the OCME, the Office of the Chief Medical Examiner.

Halfway up the block, Tawanda Jones and a dozen or so supporters are recording a video.

"Four hundred and fourteen days," Jones says to the camera. "It don't take that kind of time to do anything. It didn't take 414 days for my brother to be brutally murdered, and it shouldn't take 414 days for us to receive his whole entire autopsy report. Shame on you, medical examiner's office, Goldfarb, and all of y'all."

The camera pans to Shirley Anderson, Tyrone West's mother. "The medical examiner's office had my son's body," she says. "They took six months to come back with foolishness that my son had a heart attack. They missed all the key points. My son was beaten to death by ten to fifteen police officers . . . They beat my son. They omitted blunt-force trauma, asphyxiation from all the macing they did to him, tasing him, which caused his heart to stop beating. All of that was not mentioned in the report. They expect my family to accept that my son died of a heart attack? My son was healthy! He was healthy, make no mistake . . . Our problem with the medical examiner is, we know they're hiding facts."

Jones gestures toward me, a middle-aged white guy in the background who looks like a befuddled roadie for Jimmy Buffett's band.

"Get him on camera," Anderson says.

I only learned this later, watching the video posted to YouTube by the community activist organization Baltimore BLOC. I didn't notice them on the sidewalk until Jones walked toward me holding a sign reading ONE YEAR LATER NO COMPLETE AUTOPSY.

Sigh. It's a Wednesday. A West Wednesday.

Standing with Jones and other members of Tyrone West's family is Duane "Shorty" Davis, a diminutive man with long dreadlocks and wearing a yellow reflective vest. Davis is an activist known for decorating toilets with newspaper clippings, political statements, and other odds and ends and leaving them around town. A few years ago, he was charged — and acquitted — of making a fake explosive device after placing one of his political art toilets in front of the Baltimore County courthouse. His provocations, in my mind, are harmlessly amusing. I'm tempted to tell Shorty that I'm a fan of his toilet work. We have a mutual friend, the cartoonist Tom Chalkley. That's Smalltimore, as locals call it: the small-town connections that occur unexpectedly often in this big city.

I wish Shorty and I were friends. He's an interesting and creative person. Chalkley told me that Shorty makes the best barbecue in Baltimore. I've always wanted to try his cooking. Under other circumstances maybe we could have been friends. That is unlikely now with this invisible line drawn between us.

My friends enviously tell me I have the greatest job ever. Maybe sometimes it is. I'm not sure they'd feel the same if they knew what the work really entailed. At the moment, despite the casual attire, I am a public official. I am the bad guy.

As the protesters approach, I make sure to remain within range of the video cameras overhead. I'm not at all concerned for my safety. I've met with the West family and their supporters many times in the past. Being monitored at the OCME is just standard operational security. The conversation may be uncomfortable, but uncomfortable conversations are a routine part of my job. Whatever is about to happen, I rely on rules of engagement that have guided me in the two years that I have been executive assistant to the chief medical examiner for the state of Maryland and as public information officer, the public face of the OCME.

Don't take it personally. They are angry at larger issues, of which I am just a convenient symbol. They aren't angry at me as an individual. There is no reason to feel attacked or threatened. Don't argue. Keep it cool.

This much is not in dispute: Tyrone West died on July 18, 2013, while in the custody of police. For many Baltimoreans, West was yet another victim of excessive force that plagues the zero-tolerance, stop-and-frisk police tactics instituted under former mayor Martin O'Malley. West's family and their supporters have staged protests at various locations around town — the state's attorney's office, police headquarters, city hall, the OCME — every Wednesday without fail since then. They are as resolute as ever to seek justice.

To me and the rest of the OCME, West is case number 13-6003.

Holding her homemade cardboard sign, Jones addresses me directly. "You said that's my brother's full autopsy report, correct?"

"Right," I reply.

The complete autopsy report was published by the Baltimore Sun. *The whole report is available online. The Baltimore City State's*

Attorney's Office shouldn't have released the report to reporters.
That's a violation of COMAR, the Code of Maryland Regulations.
Section 10.35.01.14: "An individual, other than the custodian of the
records of the Office of the Chief Medical Examiner or a designee,
may not copy or distribute the official report of the Office of the
Chief Medical Examiner." Oh well.

"If that's the full autopsy report," Jones says, "what in the
world is my attorney subpoenaing right now, as we speak?"

The case file. We've had this conversation several times. That's
fine. We can go over it again, but the answers are still the same.

According to COMAR, the autopsy report is a public record
unless a case is under investigation by any agency or pending
criminal charges. The autopsy report is evidence, Dr. David R.
Fowler — the chief, the boss, the big enchilada, the alpha and
omega, the final word — lectured to me many times. In our criminal justice system, evidence is kept confidential. All other items
in a case file — investigator report, notes, sketches, photos, other
documents — are medical records under state and federal law.
"Individual files of the Chief Medical Examiner are not public
records but are private medical records protected from disclosure," according to COMAR. While the autopsy report is public,
"requests for other information or material shall be accompanied
by a court order or subpoena."

The sanctity of that case file — Tyrone West's medical record
— is guarded as diligently as it is for every one of the twelve thousand investigations the OCME conducts each year. This is true
no matter who demands it, even a grieving and angry sibling,
however righteous the cause.

On the day 223 West Wednesday protest, back in February, we
spent the better part of an hour going over this same ground,
lingering on the sidewalk in front of the OCME long after work
hours. While the sun ebbed to twilight on that chilly afternoon,
the West family and I talked about the autopsy report and case

file, Tyrone West's personal effects, and other concerns they expressed. It's all on video posted to YouTube. Anticipating the family's objection to the medical examiner's findings, I gave them a printed copy of the state law outlining the process to challenge the cause and manner of death rulings. Maryland is the only state with an appeals process written into law.

We parted that February evening on friendly terms. "You're showing some concern for the West family," George Peoples, Tyrone West's uncle, said to me. Tawanda Jones told me that out of all the government agencies — the police, the state's attorney's office, and the others — I was the only person willing to meet with the family and answer their questions. She shook my hand. "Thank you so much," Jones said. "We really appreciate that."

Today the mood is decidedly different. It has been 414 days since Tyrone West's death. The patience of the protesters is wearing thin. Tawanda Jones has a steamroller way of speaking, a torrent of outrage spilling from her lips. So I lean my aching back against the handrail and wait for her to pause.

Don't interrupt.

". . . If somebody in your family was brutally murdered," Jones said, "and you knew it was being covered up . . . He loved me. I could have been with him. I probably would have been in here, too . . . He was brutally tased, pepper-sprayed, maced, kicked, stomped. There was eleven to fifteen [police officers] on one unarmed man . . . He was born in this world with a birth certificate, and he has to have dignity leaving this crazy world . . . How in the hell is it undetermined when you have eleven to fifteen officers on one man . . ."

Hold up. That isn't what happened. But this is not the time to make that point. I'm just waiting for a ride home.

A man wearing a black leather hat, whom I'd never seen at one of these West Wednesdays before, stepped forward to question me.

"Your office subsumed the duties of the coroner?"

"Right," I say. "There haven't been coroners in Maryland since 1939."

"So your office does the coroner's inquest?" he asks.

"We don't do inquests in Maryland."

"When did the law change and you stopped it?"

"Nineteen thirty-nine."

"I was not aware of that."

"Well, you can look it up. The Medical Examiner Act of 1939."

The man held his hand to his chin, formulating his thoughts. "So you're saying you can't determine the cause of death?"

"No, the manner of death is undetermined, not the cause of death," I say.

"Now, this man was clearly beat to death." He spoke slowly. "You say you can't determine whether he was beat to death?"

He cocked his head and swept his arm in a wide arc. "If all these people beat you, right now, to death, do you think this office would come up with a determination you were beat to death?"

Look, I'm just waiting for my ride.

"This man was clearly beat to death," he continues. "And if we beat your ass to death . . ."

"Ten of us!" somebody in the crowd yells.

". . . right now, wouldn't they know you were beat to death? Let's make it personal."

I think we're about done here.

"If you're going to lie for the police," he says, "just be man enough to say you're going to lie."

Fuck the police.

Not that I have anything against cops. I've come to know many homicide detectives, crime scene technicians, city and state police, FBI, NCIS, Secret Service, and law enforcement officers of all stripes. Most are decent people and dedicated professionals. But the public gets a skewed view of the relationship between police and medical examiners from procedural crime dramas. We aren't on the same team. The police may be in charge of the scene, but their authority ends at the chalk outline around a dead body. The person within that chalk outline is the jurisdiction of the medical examiner. Any number of agencies may be involved in investigating a sudden death — police, fire department arson investigators, adult protective services, child fatality review team, OSHA, National Transportation Safety Board. They do their thing, we do ours. The medical examiner — this medical examiner office — is independent and autonomous. We aren't on any team. The medical examiner's sole duty is to the deceased person. We speak for the dead.

If people only understood how unique and amazing the OCME is. Of all the medical examiner offices in the country, there are a few of particular renown. Boston, where the medical examiner system began in 1877. New York City, one of the cradles of forensic medicine and the birthplace of forensic toxicology under the tenure of Charles Norris and Alexander Gettler. Los Angeles, where for years Thomas Noguchi was the coroner to the Hollywood stars and inspiration for Quincy, M.E. Las Vegas, the model for CSI: Vegas.

But the OCME of Maryland has always held a special place in forensic medicine. The first centralized, statewide medical examiner system in the United States. The OCME of Maryland has an unblemished reputation for excellence stretching back decades, free of the scandals and drama so common in other jurisdictions.

With only four chief medical examiners in its seventy-five-year history, the OCME has a record of stability, reliability, and institutional culture rare among any sort of governmental agency anywhere in the country. Operating under the authority of an independent commission to insulate investigations from political and public influence, the OCME is considered the gold standard to which other forensic medical centers aspire. We live by our motto, "Search for Truth."

The OCME's seventeen board-certified forensic pathologists are some of the best in the country. Maryland's forensic medical center is a highly competitive training site for six medical schools in the Baltimore-Washington area. Cause and manner of death determinations are made through a rigorous consensus process by a group of medical examiners, with layers of supervision and review for quality control.

The OCME conducts twelve thousand investigations a year, each given the same thoroughness and diligence. The agency works with two hundred or so different police departments and at least twenty-six state's attorney's offices across Maryland. How exactly would a conspiracy work? Somebody asks, "Do us a favor and overlook the broken neck"? What's the incentive? What sort of leverage could a city police department have over a state agency? They'll ticket our cars?

A forensic pathologist spends at least thirteen years in training and typically ends up with hundreds of thousands of dollars in student loan debt before the first day on the job. Do you really think a medical examiner would throw away a career for some overly aggressive local cop? Who in their right mind would deliberately fudge facts in a case that will be in the public record and contested in an open court, where the autopsy report and case file will be in the hands of adversarial defense lawyers and expert witnesses paid big bucks to tease out the most trivial of errors and smallest of discrepancies? The idea is absurd.

I'd love to talk about any of this. But I'm just trying to get home.

This West Baltimore street corner is far from Amherst, New York, the predominantly white and affluent suburb of Buffalo where I grew up. Baltimore seduced me with its charms when the city adopted me in 1982, a restless EMT/paramedic not yet detoured into a journalism career that sustained me, more or less, until my present job at the OCME. Except for a temporary exile in East Baltimore, most of my work and living experience has been in this Southwest Baltimore community known by locals as Sowebo. My first residence in the city was nearby on Lombard Street, in Union Square, across the park from 1524 Hollins Street, the row house where H. L. Mencken lived most of his life. Neighbors included the Hollins Market — the oldest of Baltimore's five public markets — the B&O Railroad Museum, and Edgar Allan Poe's house and grave.

I was enchanted by the textures of city life, the simple and elegant brick row houses, the way the streets came alive in the summertime as people gathered on marble steps to escape the heat, the echoes of bells and hoofbeats as produce peddlers — arabbers, they call them — walked colorful horse-drawn wagons, hawking their goods with a slow singsong chant: "Strawwww-berries . . . bluuuuueberries . . . waaaatermelon . . . banaaaanas . . ."

Since then, I've watched Sowebo slump into dilapidation, denied the development funds and support that revitalized the city's waterfront. While former industrial areas and working-class neighborhoods were reshaped by gentrification, West Baltimore festered into snaggletoothed blocks of vacant row houses. A heat map of vacant housing shows a dense blotch metastasizing over West Baltimore, the neighborhoods through which I commute every day. There are about thirty-three hundred vacant residences in this zip code, many so dangerously structurally unstable they are marked with signs — a white cross on a red background — warning that not even police or fire personnel will enter in an emergency.

Some blocks resemble the thinly fictionalized hell on earth depicted in *The Wire*, an open-air drug den known as Hamster-dam. Driving on McHenry Street to and from work, one of my favorite routes, there are blocks where the arabber's melodious call has been replaced by corner boys standing in the street offering roadside service, openly touting drugs with staccato urgency: "Prime Time! Prime Time! Prime Time!"

The unemployment rate in the OCME's neighborhood hovers around 50 percent. About 45 percent of the residents in the 21223 zip code live below the poverty line. More than half didn't finish high school. It is also one of the most violent and deadly neighborhoods in America. This is one of the communities in which Baltimore's violence is concentrated, with a non-fatal shooting rate more than three times the citywide average. More than two hundred people are murdered in Baltimore every year, one of the highest per-capita murder rates in the country. In Southwest Baltimore, the homicide rate among youth under twenty-five years of age is fifty-three per hundred thousand residents, more than ten times the national average. Every one of the victims, along with every other sudden or unattended death that occurs in the state of Maryland, goes through the doors of the OCME.

Despite the heartaches, this is the city I love.

I trained as an emergency medical technician in Memphis and worked for Medic Ambulance Service, which was contracted to provide emergency medical services in Shelby County. Within the city of Memphis, the work was mostly non-emergency transports, taking patients home from hospitals or transferring them between facilities. In Medic's coveted posts at suburban and rural stations, the action included medical emergencies, gunshots, agricultural injuries, and a lot of motor vehicle crashes.

As a new hire I was assigned to Medic's midtown headquarters. The office was equipped with a full kitchen, a rec room with a pool table and pinball machines, and several dormitory-like rooms where crews slept. We were on duty ninety-six hours a week, with two evenings and one twenty-four-hour period off each week. Most crews lived at Medic full-time, making the company their home. Because we essentially lived rent-free, our primary expenses were food and cigarettes. We often played cash poker between calls. Many who worked there used alcohol and marijuana when off-duty and often indulged in pharmaceuticals.

Two of the dispatchers visited several doctors to acquire a steady supply of diet pills — white cross amphetamines — to help crews work through the night.

My first partner was named Randy. We rode in a Cadillac Miller-Meteor Criterion, essentially a modified high-top hearse with deep, black leather bucket seats and a muscular engine that felt like driving a jet-powered lounge chair. Randy installed an eight-track sound system. My fondest memory of those days is racing down nighttime Memphis streets with lights swirling around us like a disco ball, Peter Frampton's live album blasting from the speakers, and sirens wailing overhead.

The guys at Medic played pranks, and as the new meat it was my turn to be victimized. Randy and I stopped along with another crew for lunch one Friday at a Shoney's, which had all-you-can-eat fried fish on the menu. I love fried fish. I ate the two fillets and fries and a side salad. The fillets were delicious; I asked for two more and ate those. I was quite full.

"You can really pack food away for a skinny guy," said Ron, the driver of the other ambulance crew.

"I like fried fish," I said.

Ron pulled a five-dollar bill from his pocket and placed it on the table. "I have five bucks that says you can't eat two more pieces of fish," he said. "No way you can eat that much."

"Don't do it," Randy said. But five dollars is five dollars, and I like fried fish. I asked for two more fillets and finished them off. Smiling, Ron handed me the money. I was uncomfortably distended, straining at my uniform belt, but pleased by my accomplishment.

"Six pieces of fish is really impressive," Ron said. "Now you're going to pick up a dead body."

"What? No. You're kidding, right?"

"Nope," Ron said. "You're next up. Have fun."

"I told you not to do it," Randy said.

Medic Ambulance had what they called a corpse removal contract with the City of Memphis. When a person was found dead, recovered after a fire or floating in a body of water, killed in a car crash or homicide, Medic was paid $25 per body to transport from the scene to the emergency room of John Gaston Hospital for official pronouncement by a doctor and then around the corner and down a ramp to the Shelby County Morgue, where Dr. Jerry Francisco presided as medical examiner. The same ambulances for sick and injured patients were used to transport the dead.

Driving to the scene, my sense of trepidation intensified. I'd never been taught anything about the dead, only how to care for living patients. Nobody trained me for this. I didn't want to do it.

"Isn't there somebody who handles this sort of thing?" I asked Randy.

"We *are* the people who handle this sort of thing," he said.

My first dead body was a homeless man in his forties on the second floor of a vacant building within blocks of Beale Street. He was prone on the floor with his left arm outstretched, which remained in position as we rolled him onto his back and made it difficult to strap the body to the gurney. It was my first experience with rigor mortis, my first touch of cold, clammy, dead human flesh. I was twenty-one years old and felt like my belly was about to burst.

Like a first kiss, you remember your first dead body. It is unsettling. Then you get used to it.

As an EMT, I saw lives dramatically altered in an instant. All it takes is a fleeting lapse of attention, a momentary distraction, an act of poor judgment. Or no fault of your own. You can be minding your own business, a whole and intact person one minute, and in the next moment you are facing prolonged medical care, disfiguring injuries, loss of a limb, a lifetime of disability. Every day on an ambulance teaches the fragility of life.

In time, I had my fill of being woken in the middle of the night for non-emergency calls. The local community college began a two-year paramedic degree program, and I was admitted into the second group of students. Despite graduating top of my class, my efforts at landing a job as a paramedic were stymied. The only EMS service in the region with the equipment and resources to provide advanced life support was the Memphis Fire Department, and in order to work for them as a paramedic a person had to attend the fire academy, work as a firefighter, and bid for an ambulance position against guys with more seniority. I didn't want to be a firefighter.

For a year I worked as an EMT for the West Memphis Fire Department across the river in Arkansas. They weren't equipped for advanced life support, but at least I didn't have to train as a firefighter. I also learned that there wasn't much in the way of a career ladder for a young EMT with ambitions. The big promotion I had to look forward to, if I played my cards right and waited for many years, was a bump up to driver. I could move over on the front seat. I wanted more than that.

Other paramedics were getting degrees in nursing, opening up opportunities for employment in emergency departments and academia. So I began a two-year nursing degree program. The curriculum and clinical practice were easy. Over my years of training as an EMT, paramedic, and nurse, I held a variety of jobs in hospitals. I drew blood, ran EKGs, worked in clinical laboratories, even worked in psychiatric units. But throughout nursing school, the basic science interested me far more than the practical duties of nursing. In my last semester, I dreaded the prospect of graduating and working as a nurse.

At a holiday party at my nursing instructor's home, another guest mentioned a book titled *Shock-Trauma*, about pioneering trauma surgeon R Adams Cowley's Baltimore "death lab" where he and his team monitored critically injured patients as they succumbed to lethal shock and developed treatments to halt the downward spiral toward death. Cowley coined the concept of the "golden hour" — the critical time period when lives can be saved — and created the country's first statewide trauma system. This was the future of emergency medicine.

Within three months, I sold everything I owned and moved to Baltimore, a place entirely unfamiliar to me.

The Maryland Institute for Emergency Medical Services Systems, the statewide EMS authority created by Cowley, began an undergraduate program in emergency health services (EHS) at the University of Maryland's Baltimore County campus. The program was designed to train paramedic managers and researchers, to create a new step in the EMS career ladder. I was accepted into the second group of students.

While registering for classes, I encountered a problem. I had already taken all of the degree requirements except for the core EHS curriculum, but I needed one more class to have enough hours to remain eligible for financial aid. Standing in line at the registration counter, I quickly leafed through the course catalog until my eyes fell on a three-credit independent study with a *Baltimore Sun* reporter. Sure, why not. I'd been fiddling around with writing in Memphis. Maybe I could learn some things.

The reporter for my independent study was Tom Nugent, a news and feature writer with a reputation, I would come to learn, as the wild man of journalism. In our freewheeling hour-long sessions, Nugent and I discussed storytelling and reporting, the craft of writing. I began contributing to the UMBC student paper, *The Retriever*. Nugent suggested that I do an internship at the Associated Press, where I learned about the inverted pyramid, attribution, AP style, and other newswriting essentials.

I got lucky with a couple of freelance assignments — a segment for NPR's *All Things Considered* about the mysterious stranger who visits Edgar Allan Poe's grave on the anniversary of his birth and an interview for *The Washington Post* with radar operator Jacob Beser, the only crew member at both Hiroshima and Nagasaki — and I began to build a portfolio.

Settling into a row house in the Union Square neighborhood across the park from Mencken's house, I was introduced to steamed crabs and other Baltimore traditions by a couple of brothers who lived a few doors up the street, Dale and Bobby Thieler. The Thielers were streetwise former juvenile delinquents, decent working-class people. Dale was married to his high school sweetheart, Michelle, and had a toddler daughter, Samantha. Bobby had been out of the navy a couple of years and worked as a mechanic.

The Thielers treated me like another brother. I spent many weekend nights and nearly every holiday — New Year's, July 4, Memorial Day, and Labor Day — with the Thielers, their family and friends, often including one of Dale's best friends, Douglas Candeloro, who went by Porky. While Dale worked the grill, we'd sit around a picnic table the boys had stolen from a state park years before, carving our names into the heavy planks of wood.

Sometimes Dale and I and a couple of others hunted rats. We'd sit on the back porch with pellet guns, scouting the alley with a flashlight, doing our part to rid the city of vermin. We also often played chess. Samantha would sit on my lap, and I'd talk in silly voices and make her laugh. She is practically my niece, and our relationship endures to this day.

At our gatherings, it wasn't uncommon for somebody to score Ecstasy or Percocet, or reveal a small folded paper containing white powder. My own choice of intoxicants is limited to occasional alcohol and marijuana. The notion of consuming an unidentified powder of unknown concentration or a random pharmaceutical of unknown provenance is a hard pass for me. So I'd politely decline, and the party would go on.

Two courses I took in the emergency health services program at UMBC fundamentally changed my thinking about trauma — Epidemiology of Injury and Injury Control. Both courses relied heavily on the work of Susan Baker, a pioneering injury epidemiologist and founding director of the Center for Injury Research and Policy at the Johns Hopkins Bloomberg School of Public Health.

Baker and her collaborators, mainly Brian O'Neill and William Haddon of the Insurance Institute for Highway Safety, developed the study of trauma as a public health matter, like an infectious disease. As with an infectious disease, trauma results from the interaction of a host, a vector, and an active agent. Calling an injury or death the result of an accident is misleading. An accident is an unpredictable random event. Things like car crashes, house fires, or unintentional poisonings aren't unpredictable or random.

Although Baker is hardly a household name, her work has touched millions of Americans. As a young postgraduate student working at Maryland's OCME, she raised the alarm on the disproportionate risk of infants and young children in car crashes, which led to the adoption of child safety seat laws in every US state. She has produced groundbreaking work on fatalities related to aviation and motorcycles, the influence of alcohol on homicide, falls among the elderly, and a wide range of other areas.

Injury control recognizes that factors before, during, and after an event can significantly alter the outcome. The most obvious example of where injury control measures have been successfully incorporated is traffic safety, everything from Jersey barriers that prevent head-on collisions and dissipate the energy of out-of-control vehicles to energy-absorbing designs of cars and trucks, seat belts, and air bags. Roads are engineered better, with improved lighting and lines of sight. Vehicles built today have fewer hazards on the dashboard and are better able to prevent intrusion into the passenger compartment. Traffic fatality rates have plummeted since the 1950s because of these improvements.

While the care that paramedics and EMTs render in the field after catastrophic events is well and good, preventing catastrophic events and mitigating their effects when they occur leads to a far greater reduction in deaths and disability.

I was considering pursuing a master's degree in public health, perhaps at Baker's Injury Research and Policy program at Johns Hopkins. I thought it might be where I could merge my interests in media and injury control and have the greatest influence by focusing on public awareness and education. Instead, when I graduated from UMBC, I took a job as public information officer for the University of Maryland School of Medicine.

My freelance writing flourished; I contributed to local and national magazines and newspapers. I began writing a column on clinical research for an emergency medical services magazine, branched out into feature stories for medical trade magazines, and eventually wrote regularly for *USA Today* and other national publications. Not bad for an ex-paramedic with no formal training.

One story altered my life in an unpredictable way. I wrote about a collection of dioramas known as the Nutshell Studies of Unexplained Death housed at the OCME of Maryland. The Nutshells were created by the independently wealthy Frances Glessner Lee, the mother of forensic science and a major figure in the field. I knew Dr. John Smialek, the chief medical examiner, from when I worked for the School of Medicine. In 1986, when Smialek held a press conference to announce the cause of basketball star Len Bias's death — cocaine intoxication — I was dispatched to the medical examiner office to help manage the throng of national and local media that descended on the OCME.

Smialek was kind enough to spend time with me talking about the Nutshells and let me borrow some images to accompany my article for *American Medical News*, the weekly newspaper of the American Medical Association. The story was a good clip, a nice addition to my portfolio, and after its publication I thought I was done with the Nutshells. But I was wrong. Friends started asking me to arrange visits with the dioramas. I became a familiar face to Linda Thomas, the OCME front desk receptionist, as I returned once or twice a year to see the Nutshells.

During one of these visits with my oldest brother, a resident of Toronto, we bumped into Smialek, a Toronto native. I introduced them and stood by as they talked at length about their favorite haunts. As my brother and Smialek chatted, my eyes wandered to three rows of photographs mounted on the wall, portraits of every medical examiner who had served at the OCME since its founding, forty-eight framed photos in all. When David Simon filmed *Homicide: Life on the Street* and *The Wire*, using the real autopsy room as a set after hours, these portraits served as a visual cue to let viewers know they were at the medical examiner office.

One of the photos looked peculiar. I leaned in for a better look. That was . . . Jack Klugman. The label read, DR. J. QUINCY, 1976–1980. Nice.

In 2012, I was an editor for *Patch*, a network of hyperlocal news sites that was owned at the time by AOL–Huffington Post. The concept of *Patch* was to provide wall-to-wall coverage in a limited neighborhood, everything from murders and fires to school sports and community group meetings. My territory was Arbutus, a community in the southwest corner of Baltimore County.

Through *Arbutus Patch*, I met Mike Eagle. Bald with a bushy mustache, Eagle has broad shoulders and a military presence. He served in the army's 82nd Airborne Division. For eight years he was assigned to the mortuary affairs unit of the Central Identification Laboratory based in Hawaii. Military people talk about leaving no man behind, and Eagle is one of the people who lived up to that motto, deploying into Vietnam, Cambodia, Laos, and other remote places around the world to recover and bring home the remains of service members.

Eagle joined the OCME in 1998 as an autopsy technician and became one of the agency's key staff. He is director of information technology at the OCME, custodian of records, and supervisor of the medical records department. I asked Eagle to lead a tour of Maryland's new state-of-the-art forensic medical center for a group of a dozen or so *Patch* editors. During our visit, Eagle mentioned that the OCME had a job opening, a new position as executive assistant to the chief medical examiner, working directly beside the boss, and public information officer for the agency. An ideal candidate, Eagle said, would be somebody with EMT experience and a journalism background.

Me, I said. That would be me.

I got the job.

When I arrived for my first day of work at the OCME, Linda Thomas, the front desk receptionist, immediately made me feel welcome.

"You don't need to sign in," she smiled. "You look like you belong here."

— CHAPTER TWO —

THE DEAD HOUSE

Progress in the dignified treatment of the dead has a complicated and colorful history in Baltimore. In the fall of 1807, a group of Baltimore physicians began offering a course of medical study that included the dissection of cadavers in an anatomical theater built at the corner of Saratoga and Liberty Streets. The first specimen acquired for anatomic study was the "waterlogged body of a criminal who drowned himself" recovered from the harbor. Among a certain anti-scientific mind-set, human dissection was considered an outrageous desecration akin to butchering. Word of abominable activities spread in the community. On the night of November 21, a mob descended on the anatomical theater. Rioters broke in and ransacked the building. They stole the partially dissected cadaver and paraded the flayed corpse down the city streets. The incident moved state lawmakers to charter the College of Medicine of Maryland — later renamed University of Maryland School of Medicine. The College of Medicine of Maryland was the fifth medical school in America, the first south of the Mason-Dixon line, and first in the nation to include the anatomical study of human cadavers in its curriculum.

The two-story domed building that served as the College of Medicine of Maryland's home was completed in 1812. Medical students watched the British bombardment of Fort McHenry sitting beneath the building's columned portico. Now known as Davidge Hall, it is the oldest medical school building continuously in use in the United States. Davidge Hall was designed with special security features to defend against the return of an angry mob. The heavy wooden front door can be braced from the inside. There are no ground-level windows to break. The cleverest feature is a spiral staircase hidden behind a false wall near the upper-floor anatomic theater, allowing students to escape out the back of the building.

The need for cadavers grew in the 1800s as medical schools multiplied. At one time, Baltimore was home to as many as seven medical schools, including what H. L. Mencken described as several "mephitic fly-by-night schools consisting principally of three or four quacks ambitious to posture as professors and a cadaver or two stolen from the Potters Field."

Grave robbing was a flourishing industry in Baltimore. The proximity of burial grounds to the Baltimore & Ohio Railroad's Mount Clare Station facilitated a brisk business providing cadavers to medical schools across the East Coast. Baltimore's reliability as a supplier of cadavers for anatomical study earned it the reputation as the Paris of America. Among those dealing in dead bodies it was known as Resurrection City.

In the formerly hidden escape staircase on the second floor of Davidge Hall, the medical school alumni association installed a small exhibit commemorating the city's grave-robbing heritage. An oak barrel of the type used to transport cadavers shares a small landing with a stainless-steel gurney, on which the dissected and mummified remains of a man affectionately known as Hermie are displayed in a Plexiglas vitrine. On the wall above the barrel is a framed reproduction of an 1830 letter from Baltimore surgery professor Dr. Nathan Ryno Smith to a colleague at Bowdoin College in Maine recording the shipment of three bodies in barrels of whiskey for a fee of $50.

"I shall immediately invoke Frank, our body-snatcher (a better man never lifted a spade), and confer with him on the matter. We can get them without any difficulty at present," Smith wrote. The letter included an itemized list of expenses. Whiskey cost 35 cents a gallon, and the barrels were $1 each. A cadaver unceremoniously unearthed without consent was worth $10.

In 1847, Baltimore passed the first law in the nation requiring a medical doctor to attend sudden and unexpected deaths when called upon by police or prosecutors. But there was nowhere to conduct an autopsy. Bodies were cursorily inspected at police stations, the undertaker's, a hospital emergency ward, or private homes. Often the dead had no proper examination at all.

Calls for the respectful treatment of Baltimore's dead became increasingly urgent. The first proposal to build "a dead house, in which to deposit dead bodies" was put forth in 1861 by Baltimore coroner Dr. Hiram Greentree, who told the city council that "the bodies of persons accidentally killed &c., are often interred in the Potter's Field, and taken therefrom to the dissecting rooms, before their friends are aware of their death, thus causing great anguish to families." No action was taken on his proposal.

The following year, Dr. Charles H. Bradford, commissioner of health and Baltimore city physician, brought up the matter of a dead house in his annual report to the mayor and city council.

> The erection of a dead house in some central and suitable location within the city, has been so often urged upon your Honorable bodies, that we should not venture to touch upon the subject, did not circumstances of almost daily occurrence so clearly demonstrate the necessity of such an institution.
>
> Under existing circumstances, the bodies of unknown persons found dead, are ordinarily carried to some of the police stations; but as there is no suitable place of deposit

at those places, they are generally removed to the public burial ground with as little delay as possible; and it not infrequently happens that the jury is had, the coffin obtained, and the body interred, even before the deceased is missed from his home; and when the body is subsequently sought for by his family or friends, it cannot always be found; such unpleasant circumstances must continue to occur so long as the city is without the convenience of a dead house, or some means by which dead bodies may be kept for a time sufficiently long for their recognition.

Scandalous stories of grave robbing prompted the General Assembly, in 1882, to establish an Anatomical Board in Baltimore City to distribute unclaimed bodies for medical education. Despite best intentions, the Anatomical Board could not provide medical schools with an adequate supply of cadavers. Grave robbing and other abuses persisted. The only known case of burking in the United States occurred in Baltimore in 1886, when a woman by the name of Emily Brown was strangled to death and her body sold for anatomic study. Her killer, John T. Ross, who worked in the dissecting room at University of Maryland School of Medicine, earned $15 for her body. The last documented grave robbing in Baltimore was in 1899.

Efforts to establish a proper morgue in Baltimore were thwarted by a lack of consensus. Some argued that the morgue should be located near the center of the city, as they were in New York and Paris. Others contended that it made more sense to place the morgue near the waterfront, because so many of the dead were victims of drowning. One proposal was for a morgue located at the former city spring property on Calvert Street between Mulberry and Lexington Streets. Residents of this upscale neighborhood objected to the presence of the morgue and the potential for traffic congestion on a major central thoroughfare.

Noting that there were five dissecting rooms in Baltimore where bodies were kept for weeks or longer without complaint, a committee of College of Physicians and Surgeons faculty sought unsuccessfully to assuage concerns of the public.

> A great deal has been said about the ineligibility of the Calvert-street spring lot for a morgue, and frightful pictures have been drawn of bloated and stinking corpses spreading consternation, disgust, and, perhaps contagion in their track, being carried through the city. One writer has even suggested that the fetid emanations from the morgue itself would render Calvert street unendurable as a place of business or residence, and even impassible to sensitive people . . .
>
> As unknown persons will be killed by railroad and other accidents, or will commit suicide by means of poison, the pistol or the rope, as well as by drowning, they will never be confined to any particular part of the city, and no matter where the morgue is located some portion of the city must be traversed in conveying them to it . . .
>
> Wherever a morgue may be located some opposition will inevitably be around among those living in that particular neighborhood.

In May 1887, the Baltimore City Council passed an ordinance to establish a morgue but appropriated no funds for its construction.

The need for a modern morgue became desperate.

"In the name of the afflicted friends of the unknown dead, in the name of our efficient and zealous police force, and in the name of every reflecting citizen of Baltimore, I urge that this long felt want shall no longer be neglected and laid aside as a matter for future consideration," city health commissioner Dr. James A. Steuart said in 1888. "A city of five hundred thousand people cannot afford to be without a Morgue anymore than she can be without electric lights."

Progress finally arrived in 1890, when the city council passed an ordinance to appoint two doctors to serve as medical examiners for the city and appropriated $4,000 to select "a suitable site on the water front, or easy access from the harbor, and cause to be erected thereon a building to be used as a morgue or dead house."

The site selected for the morgue was the eastern side of Baltimore's inner harbor, in the lumber district of the waterfront at the foot of President Street, adjacent to the mouth of the Jones Falls, an eighteen-mile-long flood-prone stream used for commercial navigation as well as a conduit for the city's open sewers. Lined with slaughterhouses, tanneries, and other businesses dumping waste into the stream, the Jones Falls was a malodorous cesspool of filthy water. The Jones Falls effluvium and various waterfront aromas would provide olfactory camouflage for the morgue's operation.

When completed in 1890, the two-story sand brick building had an autopsy room, a storage room for surgical instruments, an office, a room for holding coroner inquests, and an icebox with a capacity of eight bodies. The building was too small for a growing city. With such limited cold storage, morgue workers were forced to stack two or three bodies on a tray intended for one. Complaints were raised within a decade.

"The building now used as a morgue is entirely inadequate and serves very poorly for the purposes intended," coroner Dr. J. Ramsey Nevitt told city officials. Nevitt related a recent incident in which the stench emanating from the morgue caused a nearby police station "to vacate, temporarily at least, their quarters, even after every precaution had been taken, including the liberal use of disinfectants."

Visiting the morgue to identify a body was an extremely unpleasant experience. In addition to the smells and sounds of a bustling waterfront, the building was often enshrouded in smoke from passing boats and trains. "The mode of access to the building and its immediate surroundings cause quite a shock to sensitive people, especially to women," Nevitt said.

In 1917, the B&O Railroad purchased the property on which the city morgue was located, and the operation was temporarily relocated to a vacated lumber warehouse across the street until a new facility could be built. This temporary relocation lasted for more than seven years.

As had happened years earlier, disagreements about a location bogged down progress on the building of a new morgue. Despite widespread agreement that a new one was absolutely essential, nobody wanted a morgue near where they worked or lived.

Conditions in the former lumber shop were abysmal. One member of the public wrote to the newspaper to describe the experience of going to the morgue to identify the husband of a friend.

> Aside from the nasty, dirty and partly dangerous section, I must say that inside the room is one of the dirtiest holes in town. There is no waiting room for ladies, no chairs to sit on if anyone should become faint and no disinfectant whatever kept in the place . . .
>
> When we viewed the body we could not help seeing other bodies, for they were all in the same compartment and mostly all exposed. Bodies that were dragged out of the river and the remains of persons who were killed and mangled in accidents, both black and white, male and

female, all were in the one part, and those that had been there for a week or more had started to decompose and the worst stench filled the room, aside from the dirty can that held the old, wet and dirty clothing that was removed from the bodies.

In 1922, a group of coroners spoke out about the conditions at the morgue. Southern district coroner Dr. George C. Blades called the temporary morgue "the worst blot on this city that I can think of." He said that "a person dropping dead in the city streets because of heat or sudden illness is brought into this terrible place and put side by side with some decomposed body that had been dragged from the water. I feel positive that if the majority of people knew of the conditions they would rise up in their ire and demand immediate correction of the evils now existing."

"We have no decent facilities for an autopsy, not half of the proper medical instruments required, no photographic room, no room for records or files, no refrigeration plant, no plant for hot water, no nightkeeper and only eight shelves on which to place the dead that come here," said at-large coroner Dr. Otto M. Reinhardt. "The place is absolutely filthy and unsanitary."

"I hate to take people into this building," morgue superintendent August H. Rittmiller told a reporter. Although he diligently hosed the premises with disinfectant, Rittmiller said that "the stench cannot be overcome in these quarters."

That same year, the city purchased property for a new purpose-built morgue, a concrete one-story building, across the street from the converted lumber warehouse next to the Eastern Avenue Pumping Station. Baltimore was one of the last American cities to install enclosed sanitary sewers; when built in 1912, the pumping station was the crown jewel of the city's sewage system.

Even before construction began, health commissioner Dr. C. Hampson Jones complained that the morgue, although modern in design, was not as large as it should be. "We should build the morgue with a view to future needs," he said.

The building at 700 Fleet Street was completed and opened in 1925. This building served as the Baltimore Morgue, and later the Office of the Chief Medical Examiner for the State of Maryland, for the next forty-four years.

The coroner system of death investigation, which still exists in about half of the United States, is a persisting relic of medieval English common law. Since the time Maryland was settled as a colony in 1632, sudden and unexpected deaths were under the jurisdiction of coroners.

Although responsible for certifying the cause and manner of death for official records, a coroner doesn't necessarily have to know anything about medicine or law. Coroners typically have been political figures elected to office, securing their positions by virtue of receiving more votes than somebody else, not because they are the most qualified. In many parts of the country, a sheriff, justice of the peace, or undertaker also serves as coroner.

Coroners in Maryland were appointed rather than elected to office. The job thus tended to be filled by loyal medical mediocrities who played well with police and prosecutors. In Baltimore, the city's coroners were medical doctors, but not necessarily good ones. A doctor with a thriving practice doesn't need the unpleasantness of postmortem examination.

By 1939, ten physicians were serving as coroners in Baltimore City. Eight were assigned to police districts, one served at-large throughout the city, and one was assigned to automotive fatalities. Elsewhere in Maryland, death investigation was uneven. Five of the state's twenty-two counties had physician coroners, while in the others a local magistrate served as coroner.

The coroner system in Baltimore — and throughout the state of Maryland — was unreliable and prone to corruption. It was entirely at a coroner's discretion whether to call a shooting a homicide or an accident. The coroner also investigated work-related deaths and was involved in many situations that could be resolved with influence or bribes. Funeral parlors lined pockets for sending business their way. As they had since colonial days, coroners were authorized to bring charges — or not — in cases of homicide, a situation that tempted abuse.

Coroners were unsupervised and unaccountable. They were slow to submit reports to the health department and the state's attorney and unreliable witnesses in court. Coroners had the option of sending a body to the city morgue for autopsy but were more likely to list on the death certificate whatever fanciful diagnosis came to mind, with little regard for the dead person or the facts.

"It's a known fact that the old system of 'coroner's' diagnosis is replete with guesses, snapshot diagnoses based often on hearsay and without personal investigation," said Dr. Howard J. Maldeis, postmortem physician at the city morgue.

Members of the state medical society, the Medical and Chirurgical Faculty of Maryland, or MedChi, accused coroners of engaging in racketeering. When reform-minded former Baltimore City state's attorney Herbert O'Conor was elected governor in 1938, MedChi seized the opportunity to transform the investigation of sudden, unexpected, and suspicious deaths in Maryland. As a former prosecutor, O'Conor appreciated the deficiencies of the coroner system.

The medical society formed a committee to draft legislation for a radically different approach to death investigation, replacing coroners with a statewide medical examiner system. In the proposed legislation, a chief medical examiner trained in the emerging field of forensic pathology would be given independent authority over death investigation. The medical examiner's responsibility would be to the decedent, not the police or prosecutors.

The chief medical examiner would be based at the Baltimore morgue, the primary site of autopsies for Baltimore City and the five closest counties in the metro area, and provide laboratory services and expertise throughout the state. The central Baltimore office would also store records and specimens.

The MedChi committee borrowed some of the best features of the laws governing medical examiner offices in New York City and Newark, New Jersey, and incorporated innovative ideas of their own. To keep the forensic investigations insulated from political influence and public pressure, the proposed law placed the Office of the Chief Medical Examiner under the governance of an independent Postmortem Examiners Commission. Composed of the chairman of pathology at University of Maryland and Johns Hopkins medical schools, the director of the state department of health, the commissioner of the Baltimore City Health Department, and the attorney general of Maryland, the Postmortem Examiners Commission would have sole authority over the chief medical examiner. Much like an executive board, the commission would be responsible for hiring and firing medical examiners, approving policies and procedures, and all the operational activity of the OCME. Any major decision, such as hiring the chief medical examiner, required a majority vote of commission members.

The Medical Examiner Act went into effect on June 1, 1939. Maldeis, who had served as postmortem physician at the Baltimore Morgue for two decades, was appointed by the Postmortem Examiners Commission as the first chief medical examiner for the state of Maryland.

Maldeis forged a statewide medical examiner system from a patchwork of jurisdictions, transforming the former city morgue — now the Office of the Chief Medical Examiner — into a capable centralized forensic facility. He improved and expanded the morgue's laboratory, adding a part-time toxicologist and a technician to the staff, and introduced photography as a routine part of forensic investigation.

At last, the public could be assured of a competent medical examination by a professional independent of the police and the state's attorney. The chief medical examiner represents the public interest, divorced from politics and the criminal justice system. The relationship between the medical examiner and the deceased is as sacred as any doctor–patient relationship, with the same ethical and legal obligations.

"One of the most important duties of the chief medical examiner is to protect those concerned after the demise of a loved one, and to see that they are dealt with honestly," Maldeis said.

Nearly a decade into the new position, Maldeis developed pancreatic cancer that metastasized to his liver. He continued to work nearly to his final days as the disease ravaged his body, until his death on January 15, 1949.

A search for a successor to Maldeis began soon after his death. The Postmortem Examiners Commission oversaw an innovative statewide system and wanted a progressive, well-qualified chief to lead the agency. At the time, there were very few pathologists trained in medicolegal or forensic pathology in the United States.

On a warm evening in May 1949, members of the Postmortem Examiners Commission met at the Elkridge Country Club outside Baltimore with the grande dame of forensic science, Frances Glessner Lee, and her friend Erle Stanley Gardner, best-selling author of Perry Mason novels. Known as Captain Lee, the millionairess grandmother used her fortune to establish the country's first academic department of legal medicine at Harvard Medical School.

After dinner, the discussion turned to the vacancy at the OCME. Lee praised a young pathologist who had recently completed his three-year fellowship in Harvard's Department of

Legal Medicine, Dr. Russell Fisher. "He's going places," she told the commission. "He's competent, conscientious, and has a lot of innate executive ability." On Lee's advice, the commission appointed Fisher as chief medical examiner, a position he held for the next thirty-five years.

Privately, Lee described Fisher as a "live wire" to the advisory board of her legal medicine foundation. She feared he could be a potential rival of the program she had founded at Harvard. "Dr. Fisher is a go-getter," she told her advisory board. "He will have a Department of Legal Medicine established in Baltimore which could seriously jeopardize the success of ours at Harvard, so must be watched."

The sensational 1952 murder of Dorothy May Grammer cemented Fisher's reputation as a medical detective. Just after midnight on August 20, a patrol car with two police officers had just turned west on Taylor Avenue in the Parkville community of Baltimore County when a Chrysler careened past them at high speed, clipping a telephone pole and launching into the air, then flipping over and landing on its right side. When police officers arrived at the wreck, engine still racing and wheels spinning, the vehicle's occupant was dead.

Grammer, a thirty-three-year-old Sunday school teacher, had just dropped her husband, Edward, at the train station, where he was traveling to New York City for work. At first the crash seemed like a tragic accident. But some things didn't add up for Fisher. Grammer had skull fractures — caused by forces from three different directions — and several lacerations on her head, but the car sustained little damage. Nothing in the passenger compartment could account for the lacerations. Blood was noted on the driver's seat but not on the passenger side where Grammer's crumpled body was found. Fisher observed numerous bruises on Grammer's body during the autopsy, which could not have been caused by the crash. It takes two or more minutes for blood to coagulate and form a bruise, but police were at the crash within seconds and found her dead.

"I said, uh-uh, this doesn't fit," Fisher recalled to a newspaper reporter later in his career. "She's got too many different lacerations of her head, she's got injuries that took time to swell and discolor. This doesn't happen in two or three minutes."

Fisher's examination determined that Grammer had been severely beaten and struck on the head with a weapon five times, resulting in a fatal skull fracture. Edward Grammer was charged with his wife's murder. Police accused him of beating his wife to death, then placing a pebble beneath the gas pedal to keep the accelerator wide open and staging the crash to look like an accident. Grammer was convicted of the crime and executed in 1954.

Fisher transformed the OCME into a leading center of research, education, and training in forensic pathology. He established fellowship programs in forensic pathology and toxicology. The roster of medical examiners who trained or worked under Fisher at the OCME is a who's who of forensic pathology: Charles S. Hirsch of New York City, Joseph H. Davis of Miami-Dade County, Ronald N. Kornblum of Los Angeles, Vincent Di Maio of San Antonio, and Charles S. Petty of Dallas, who once said, "Dr. Fisher has trained more people in forensic pathology than anybody else in the United States."

Werner U. Spitz did his fellowship under Fisher's supervision and served as deputy chief of the OCME. Spitz and Fisher co-authored *Medicolegal Death Investigation*, often referred to as the bible of forensic pathology and still regarded as a standard reference. Appointed chief medical examiner in Detroit in 1972, Spitz recast the office in the mold of the OCME of Maryland.

Fisher engaged in a range of research projects in collaboration with the Hopkins School of Public Health, University of Maryland School of Medicine and hospital, the Armed Forces Institute of Pathology, and the National Institutes of Health. Among the areas in which the OCME made important contributions are studies of crib death, heart attacks, vehicular crashes and trauma, and drowning.

"Dr. Fisher was very broad-minded," Susan Baker said. "He gave me access to anything I needed. There was interest in what I was doing and willingness on the part of Dr. Fisher and the other assistant medical examiners and residents to help me in my research. They were happy to see the results of their work going to someplace other than a file cabinet."

Within a few years of his arrival at the OCME, Fisher was generating upward of $100,000 annually in research grants, which he used through the private nonprofit Maryland Medico-Legal Foundation to fund salaries and equipment for the OCME. The outside support was essential to augment the meager funding provided by the State of Maryland, amounting to about $140,000 annually in the mid-1950s. "Less than the money it takes for the game department to stock fish in our lakes," Fisher once complained to a newspaper reporter.

The OCME of Maryland earned a sterling reputation for training, research, and forensic death investigation. "No matter where you go throughout the United States, when you discuss legal medicine and the efficiency with which unexplained deaths are checked, homicides investigated and facts placed in the hands of the prosecuting attorney, you find that Baltimore and Maryland rank right up in the top grouping of the top bracket," Erle Stanley Gardner wrote, dedicating his 1952 Perry Mason novel, *The Case of the Moth-Eaten Mink*, to Fisher.

As the 1960s approached, it became increasingly apparent that the aging Fleet Street morgue was obsolete and inadequate for the needs of a modern medical examiner office. "The Fleet Street building was primitive in many ways," Susan Baker said. "It was cramped and crowded."

The decrepit building, next to a sewage pumping station along Baltimore's derelict waterfront, hardly matched the prestige contained within. When Spitz arrived at the Fleet Street building for his fellowship in 1959, he wasn't sure whether he had made a terrible mistake.

"I was taken to a very dilapidated part of town within the harbor area of Baltimore," he said. "When the cab stopped I looked out the window and debated whether to get out or return to the hotel, until the driver pointed out the sign above the door of the building which read 'State of Maryland Medical Examiner's Office.'"

In 1962, the state acquired property near the University of Maryland medical center campus at the corner of Pratt and Penn Streets, the site of a former Anheuser-Busch warehouse. A three-story state-of-the-art medical examiner office was dedicated on September 10, 1969. Funds for the new building were earmarked from the state's racetrack revenues, supported by a $100,000 contribution from the Maryland Medico-Legal Foundation.

As an administrator Fisher was easygoing, although a stickler for following proper procedures. He left much of the day-to-day business of the OCME to his administrative supervisor, Dorothy Hartel, who ruled with sternly worded memos about timekeeping, proper work uniforms, and lunch breaks. It was understood that Fisher was the chief, but Hartel really ran the OCME.

In later years, Hartel was also Fisher's drinking companion, particularly after his wife died in 1983. Drinking alcohol aggravated Fisher's liver disease, which some suspect may have been caused by the hepatitis C virus, which wasn't identified until several years after his death. Fisher worked until illness forced his retirement. Three weeks later, on May 21, 1984, he died of liver disease at the age of sixty-seven.

The Postmortem Examiners Commission appointed Dr. John E. Smialek to continue Fisher's legacy. A native of Toronto,

Smialek received his medical degree at the University of Toronto. For three years, he was a general practitioner and coroner in Thunder Bay, Ontario.

Smialek returned to Toronto for his residency in pathology and completed a fellowship in forensic pathology under the supervision of Werner Spitz in Detroit. He remained in Detroit as an associate medical examiner, and then deputy chief, before moving to Albuquerque as the chief medical examiner for New Mexico.

Steeped in the practices of Spitz and Fisher, Smialek was an apt successor as chief of Maryland's OCME. Smialek's reputation as an authority in forensic pathology was unquestionable. He improved the OCME's investigative capabilities, expanded training programs, and introduced the computerization of records. But many of Fisher's research projects — and the funding that came with them — went by the wayside as Smialek concentrated on the OCME's core forensic investigation responsibilities.

Smialek was soft-spoken and personable but unsparing in his criticism of medical examiners who fell short of his standards. "Smialek had his own way of doing things," said Fowler, who trained under Smialek and served as his senior deputy chief. "The vast majority of medical examiners were scared shitless of him."

In 2001, the weeklong Frances Glessner Lee Homicide Investigation Seminar was held during the second week of May. On Tuesday, Smialek led the several dozen police officers in attendance through a forensic autopsy. That evening, the group went out for a fancy steakhouse banquet. The following day, on the afternoon of May 9, Smialek was at his desk looking at histology specimens — stained tissues mounted on glass slides — with another medical examiner. Without speaking, Smialek leaned backward in his chair as though stretching his back, and lost consciousness. CPR was begun and help summoned. An ambulance rushed Smialek to the University of Maryland Medical Center emergency department, two blocks away.

A distance runner who didn't smoke or drink, thought to be perfectly healthy, Smialek died of a sudden cardiac arrhythmia resulting from a myocardial infarction. He was fifty-seven years old.

— CHAPTER THREE —

BEGINNINGS

Tom Brown, the OCME's administrator, his long dark hair pulled into a ponytail, walked me to my office and gestured to my desk. That was the entirety of my orientation to the OCME on my first day on the job. No instruction or direction about what my job entailed. I had been issued a swipe card for the elevators and access to restricted areas and a master key to unlock any door in the building.

My desk was in the outer office in the chief medical examiner's suite, with a bank of bright windows overlooking the BioPark garage across Poppleton Street. Between my desk and chief medical examiner Fowler's office was a small meeting space — half a dozen chairs around a rustic wood table made from a barn door. The table once belonged to Smialek.

Fowler was out of the office, so I was left to myself to figure out what I was supposed to do. On my desk were three documents. One was my job description, known as an MS-22 form, which listed my main responsibilities: sort through and handle calls and mail directed toward the chief, serve as the chief's representative internally and externally, respond to inquiries as the public information officer, and troubleshooting.

The other two documents on my desk were Health-General, Title 5 of the Annotated Code of Maryland and Title 10 of the

Maryland Code of Regulation, or COMAR. Together, these documents define the authority and operation of the OCME. I began at the beginning.

> There is in the Department an Office of the Chief Medical Examiner . . .

I kept encountering Cindy Feldstein's name on paperwork and personal items around my work space. This used to be Feldstein's desk. She had been Fowler's secretary and served as spokesperson for the OCME. On the evening of February 11, 2011, Feldstein was crossing Park Heights Avenue against traffic and was fatally struck by a Maryland Transit Administration bus. She was fifty-three and left a husband and four children. Feldstein was brought to the OCME for an autopsy and attended to by her co-workers.

The realization dawned on me that I probably would not have this job if not for the sudden deaths of two individuals — Smialek and Feldstein.

One of the first assignments Fowler gave me was to deal with the state Office of the Inspector General over the matter of the OCME having not completed required financial disclosure forms for the preceding few years. "Throw yourself at their mercy," he told me. "Blame the disorganization on Cindy's absence. Tell them we will be in full compliance from now on."

I did as he said, and it worked. All it took was one phone call.

Nothing could prepare me for the range of things I would be handling on a daily basis. My phone rang often, calls forwarded from Investigations and the front desk about things that were out of the ordinary, matters that couldn't be handled at a lower level and might require the chief's attention: family members demanding to know why an investigation was taking so long; students wanting help with school projects; requests for autopsy reports and toxicology results; requests for a blood sample for paternity testing; distressed parents looking for missing children, calling the morgue when all of the hospitals had been exhausted.

I quickly learned my way around the computerized case management system, known as CME, which contains detailed information of every investigation. CME is the central nervous system of the organization. Developed in-house by the OCME's information technology department, CME is a sophisticated database that integrates all information and material related to investigations, from the time and location of the incident and pronouncement of death to the forensic investigator's report, toxicology testing results, PDFs of police and EMS reports, and photos from the scene and autopsy.

One button on CME lists the daily conference sheet, the list of all decedents in the building for examination that day. Each listing has the deceased person's name and age, if known, the county in which they were pronounced dead, and the medical examiner and autopsy technician assigned to the case. The listing also includes a brief narrative about the circumstances of the death: found decomposed, ejected in single-vehicle crash, history of substance abuse. The narrative may or may not ultimately be found related to death. It's just what is known at the time. The forensic investigator's report has more detailed information about the circumstances of the death and what could be pieced together at the scene.

I used CME continuously through the day as reporters called for cause and manner of death rulings for stories they were working on — car crashes, fatal fires, people found dead at home. There are limits on what information about a case can be released, and to whom.

The OCME is subject to a court order issued as a result of a lawsuit filed by *The Washington Post* for access to the agency's data under the Maryland Public Information Act. State law says that an autopsy report is a public document, but all other information in a case file is a confidential medical record that can be released only in response to a subpoena or court order. Because the autopsy report is public, the judge ruled, ten specific fields of data are also public information: name, sex, race, and age of the decedent; the name of the medical examiner assigned to the case; the county in which the death occurred; the date of death; the cause and manner of death; and the OCME case number.

Any other information is off limits. It is not public and cannot be released.

There were calls that stopped me cold. When I was still relatively new at the job, I answered a call from a man, young by the sound of his voice, who said he heard that his sister just died. He told me her name and date of birth. I checked CME, and she was on the conference sheet for the following day.

Next-of-kin notifications are supposed to be done by the police. The death was so recent they hadn't reached the family yet. What should I say? I couldn't pass this kid off to somebody else. I couldn't tell him to call the police or wait for somebody to get in touch with him. That would have been saying she was dead without saying it, cruelly prolonging his distress, the cowardly way out. He was entitled to the truth, and I had to be the one to deliver it. This became my first death notification.

"Yes, she is here," I said, adding for clarity, "She is dead."

"Oh God," he cried, his voice rising into a wail. "What do I do now?"

He hung up, leaving those words reverberating in my head. *What do I do now?* I was left wondering whether he meant in a practical sense — "How do I choose a funeral home or crematory?" Or did he mean, "How do I tell my parents that their daughter is dead?" Or "How can I go on living without her?"

Years later, I still don't have a good answer for the last one. We grieve. We adapt. Life goes on.

As I got to know the OCME staff, I was amazed by how long some people had worked there. One might expect burnout to lead to a high turnover rate at a medical examiner office. But at the OCME, this was hardly the case. Many had worked there twenty, thirty years or more.

The staff was like a family. In some cases, it was family. Two sets of mothers and daughters worked at the OCME. Linda Thomas, who sits at the front desk, is the sister of Eleanor Thomas, the OCME's education coordinator. Both have worked at the agency for years. Two of the clerks in the records department joined the OCME as young women in their twenties and have worked together for more than thirty years, through marriages, children, and grandchildren.

One of the forensic photographers, Ricky Jacobson, was hired by Russell Fisher in 1969 as a sixteen-year-old kid. His first task was moving boxes out of the old 700 Fleet Street morgue and into the new medical examiner office at 111 Penn Street, where Fisher trained him in forensic photography. It's the only job he's ever had.

The medical examiners were an eclectic bunch, seventeen board-certified forensic pathologists in all, including the chief and two deputies, trained at some of the best medical schools in the country: Johns Hopkins, Cleveland Clinic, Cornell, Duke. Many of the medical examiners had areas of expertise — infant and child deaths, ballistic wounds, toxicology, radiology.

Through thirteen years of training and education, the doctors worked hard to land their positions as assistant medical examiners at the OCME of Maryland. Some took a cut in pay, such is the OCME's prestige. They are smart, seasoned doctors at the top of their game.

All of the medical examiners were involved in the training of fellows, residents, medical school and graduate students. All of them had extensive courtroom experience being grilled by sharp defense lawyers. All of them have worked on sensational, high-profile cases.

Most of the medical examiners are women. "We have Asians, Europeans, and Americans on staff here," Fowler told me. "Men and women; Blacks and whites; Muslims, Jews, and Christians; gay and straight. This is the most diverse medical examiner office I've seen in the country."

Having known many doctors in my various careers with whom I could compare them, I respected the medical examiners immensely. And I discovered in time that we were like-minded. The processes of a forensic investigation are the same as journalism — asking questions, gathering and checking facts, separating facts from opinion, distinguishing what you know for sure from what may or may not be true. Investigating is investigating. Both professions require critical thinking and skepticism. The medical examiner's task, in essence, is to integrate the known facts into a succinct narrative explaining why a person died. An autopsy report is the last chapter of a person's life.

One of the deputy chiefs, Dr. Mary Ripple, was particularly difficult to read. She marched the floor scowling, giving off the vibe that she could erupt at any moment. "'Go fuck yourself' is her way of saying 'Good morning,'" the deputy chief of investigations told me by way of introduction. I kept my distance and approached her, with caution and deference, only when absolutely necessary.

Not all of the medical examiners welcomed my presence at the OCME. Dr. Carol Allan, one of the senior doctors, is something of a perfectionist. So controlling about the quality of her work that she cannot rely on a secretary to type up her autopsy reports, Allan writes up her own reports, and faster than any other doctor.

After meeting with the chief in his office, Allan paused on the way out and practically hissed at me, "I don't know what you're doing here."

That makes two of us, lady.

One exception was Dr. Theodore King, whose cluttered office was around the corner from mine. Not long into the job, I went to King's office so he could sign a letter.

"Let me buff this a little bit," he said, taking the paper from my hand.

"Buffing and turfing," I said. The term comes from Samuel Shem's satirical hospital classic *House of God*, a novel that also gave emergency department personnel the disparaging term *GOMER* for an unpleasant patient — Get Out of My Emergency Room.

King turned and smiled. "A fan of *House of God*?" he said. "You'll fit in well here."

After that, we got along great. Cynical until he breaks into a laugh, King has a dark and sardonic sense of humor. The son of a noted obstetrician-gynecologist and former department chair at the Johns Hopkins School of Medicine, King was raised for a career in medicine. He was considering pediatrics, he once told me, until he realized he hates working with kids.

King has the reputation of being the slowest medical examiner on the OCME's staff. He would still be doing autopsies late in the afternoon while the autopsy techs stood by with their arms folded, waiting until they could wash the floor and go home. But he was slow because he was so painstakingly meticulous, checking his findings and measuring twice. You get only one opportunity to do things right.

The chief medical examiner, my direct boss, David R. Fowler, stood at the top of the food chain. Tall and solidly built, with thinning hair and a close-clipped gray beard, he was a paternal figure respected by the medical examiners.

A native of Bulawayo, the second-largest city in what was then known as Rhodesia, now Zimbabwe, Fowler attended medical school at University of Cape Town in South Africa during the last years of apartheid. After completing a five-year residency in pathology, he moved to Baltimore with his wife, Carolyn Cump-sty Fowler, as she worked on a postdoctoral fellowship in injury prevention with Susan Baker at the Johns Hopkins School of Public Health.

After a three-year residency in anatomic pathology and a two-year fellowship in forensic pathology supervised by Smialek, Fowler had internalized OCME culture. He joined the OCME as an assistant medical examiner in 1993, eventually serving in both deputy chief positions, one of which oversees autopsy services and the medical staff; the other supervises Investigations.

The Postmortem Examiners Commission appointed Fowler acting chief after Smialek's unexpected death and a year later named him the permanent chief medical examiner. Fowler was just the fourth chief since the OCME's founding in 1939. His appointment was an assurance of business as usual, continuing the procedures and policies that had guided the OCME for more than six decades. "The health and welfare of this organization, and service to citizens, is what I focus on," Fowler said, "protecting what has been built by my predecessors."

When I joined the OCME, people were still talking about Christine Jarrett, a woman whose body had been recently recovered. Jarrett disappeared on January 3, 1991. Her husband, Robert Jarrett, said that Christine walked away from the home they shared with two young sons in Elkridge, in Howard County. Police suspected foul play, but Jarrett refused permission to search his property, and police lacked evidence to obtain a warrant. For more than twenty years the case remained open.

Jarrett remained in the Elkridge home, raised his sons, and remarried in 1993. His second attempt at matrimony failed, and in 2012 the couple separated. Jarrett moved out and was living with another woman. Police got word that his marriage was on the rocks. They went to speak with his estranged wife and asked permission to search the property. She agreed.

Police looked inside a shed in the backyard. Beneath the floor-boards was a patch of concrete. Investigators unearthed a dirty gray mass about four and a half feet long and two feet wide, a crude sarcophagus containing the remains of Christine Jarrett.

"Jarrett did a good job preserving her body for us," the OCME's forensic anthropologist, William Rodriguez, told me. His exam-ination found that the remains were of a white female in her mid-thirties, consistent with thirty-four-year-old Christine Jarrett. The absence of insect activity indicated that she was buried during a cold time of year. Christine Jarrett vanished in January. Dental records confirmed her identity.

Robert Jarrett was convicted of second-degree murder and sentenced to the maximum of thirty years in prison.

Rodriguez was one of the OCME's luminaries. A native of Memphis, he was co-founder with William Bass of the University of Tennessee Anthropological Research Facility, outside Knox-ville, better known as the Body Farm, and is recognized as an expert on decomposition and environmental forensics.

For more than two decades, Rodriguez was the chief forensic anthropologist and deputy chief medical examiner for special investigations for the Department of Defense. He was involved in body identification after the 9/11 attack on the Pentagon; dug up mass graves in Kosovo and Iraq to document war crimes; inves-tigated terrorist bombings, the USS *Cole* attack, the *Black Hawk Down* incident in Mogadishu, and the space shuttle Challenger explosion.

Dr. Juan Troncoso, one of the world's leading authorities on neurodegenerative disorders, provided neuropathology consul-tation to the OCME. Director of the Brain Resource Center at the Johns Hopkins School of Medicine, Troncoso has been asso-ciated with the OCME since 1981. Along with Fowler and another OCME medical examiner, Troncoso co-authored *Essential Forensic Neuropathology*. Dr. Renu Virmani, former chair of the

Armed Forces Institute of Pathology and an internationally renowned cardiovascular pathologist, provided cardiac pathology for the OCME.

Whatever specialist a case required, the OCME was hooked up with some of the best around. It was an all-star team of forensic investigation.

It took me awhile to get oriented to the massive and bewildering building that serves as the OCME's current home. The 120,000-square-foot, six-story facility occupies an entire city block on the edge of the BioPark, a fourteen-acre biomedical research campus adjacent to the University of Maryland Medical Center.

To a casual observer, the OCME's gleaming facade looks like an inconspicuous office building. Windows coated with reflective blue energy-efficient film angle toward the street, giving the structure a forward-leaning and vaguely aggressive profile. Nothing hints at the extraordinary world within its walls.

During the fall of 2001, on the heels of the 9/11 terrorist attacks, letters containing anthrax spores were mailed to several media offices and elected officials. Letters addressed to Senators Tom Daschle and Patrick Leahy passed through the US Postal Service's main processing facility for the District of Columbia in Brentwood, Maryland. Four workers at the facility developed inhalational anthrax, including two men who died. One forty-seven-year-old postal worker died at his Clinton, Maryland, home.

Maryland is home to many potential terrorism targets, including the National Security Agency, the Social Security Administration, the US Naval Academy, the US Army's biowarfare lab at Fort Detrick, and the Aberdeen Proving Ground. But the state was ill equipped to handle bioterrorism, mass fatalities, and other threats posed in the dawning post-9/11 era. If the Washington area was hit with a bioterror attack, there was nowhere to

conduct the autopsies safely. The thirty-year-old medical examiner office at 111 Penn Street, where the postal worker's autopsy
was conducted, had a single isolation room that was ineffective
for preventing a deadly infectious agent from escaping and killing Baltimoreans. The ceiling was a wobbly concrete slab that
wasn't airtight, and the walls had exposed porous mortar that
could not be disinfected.

The Penn Street building had long exceeded its capacity.
Twice as many cases as the building was designed to handle were
going through. The autopsy room had only three stations. Even
doubling up with two tables at each station was not enough for
the daily caseload. Facilities were so inadequate the OCME was
at risk of losing accreditation by the National Association of
Medical Examiners.

Working with a team of architects, designers, and enlightened
state officials, Fowler oversaw the construction of a new $50
million state-of-the-art facility incorporating very cool, innovative features. The first forensic medical center designed for the
post-9/11 era, the OCME is intended to anticipate anything the
state of Maryland may need for the next generation. Completed
in 2010, the OCME still felt new when I began working there two
years later. The walls, accented in a deep rich blue, were spotless.
Stainless-steel fixtures gleamed.

Public access to the building is restricted. Press a button by
the street-level entrance, and the front door clicks open. A small
foyer leads to two elevators. Without a swipe card, the only place
the elevators go is the fourth-floor reception area.

Linda Thomas, the OCME's ever-cheerful receptionist, sits at
the front desk separated from visitors by one and a half inches of
bullet-resistant Lexan atop a blast-resistant wall. Tastefully
furnished as any contemporary waiting room, the public lobby is
designed to contain violence. Two more locked reinforced doors
limit visitor access to the OCME's restricted area. Thomas

observes the entrances, sidewalks, and ground-floor receiving area on a video monitor. She clicks buttons to unlock doors and allow visitors access to the building.

Behind Thomas is a long, open sun-drenched space where forensic investigators, dressed in maroon polo shirts and black tactical pants, work at desks overlooking the picturesque round-house of the B&O Railroad Museum two blocks to the south. During the previous year 11,118 deaths, or about a quarter of all fatalities in the state, were reported to the OCME. Calls from throughout the state are answered in this room.

Funeral home vehicles enter the building through a fifteen-foot high-speed roll-up door on the west side, on Amity Street. The ground floor is large enough for three lanes of traffic. Funeral home drivers take one path to a bank of three body elevators that lead to the autopsy suite one floor above. The path to the right loops around for access to a parking area with enough room for about two dozen vehicles. A few spaces are reserved for funeral directors and OCME vehicles, and the rest are perks for the chief and a handful of department heads and key personnel. The third path is a tunnel behind the body elevators running along the back of the building to an exit roll-up door on Poppleton Street.

Like most of the building, the OCME garage was designed with dual functionality. Each area has more than one purpose. The parking garage doubles as the OCME's mass fatality area. Columns in the parking garage are equipped with electrical outlets, hot and cold water, drainage, broadband, and everything else that would be needed to convert the space into a temporary autopsy room. The doors and ceiling are tall enough to admit tractor trailers. If necessary, in a mass fatality incident, refrigerator trailers could be brought in and lined up. A decontamination tent can be set up for hazmat incidents.

The body elevators go up one floor, opening into a wide accession area. Bodies are checked in by forensic investigators at a station near the body elevator, next to a scale built into the floor. Two walk-in refrigerators, one for those arriving and the other for decedents who have been examined and are ready for release, can each hold dozens of bodies on rolling gurneys. In total, the OCME has the capacity to store about 470 bodies.

At the far end of the floor are the two main autopsy rooms, East and West. Each huge gymnasium-scaled room, two stories tall, is illuminated by a grid of fixtures with halogen bulbs that can churn out a blazing eight hundred lumens per square foot of light on the gurneys on which autopsies are performed. The lighting is designed so that no shadows are cast in the room, even when leaning over a body. With natural light from large southern-facing windows — obscured from outside view by frosted louvers — the autopsy rooms can get blindingly bright.

Each autopsy room has eight stainless-steel stations: a sink and a countertop with a small assortment of instruments and a white plastic cutting board. A hanging scale with a large stainless-steel bowl is suspended over each sink.

Next to a sterile operating room used to harvest cadaver skin and tissue for transplantation is the door leading into the biosafety suite, where bodies that are decomposed or potentially infectious are held. To design the suite, architects looked at biosafety level III laboratories operated by the federal government that handle deadly agents. "Nobody ever designed a biosafety autopsy room before," Fowler told me.

Press a plate and the door swings open to the decomp area. From this point the odor is more pungent. Powerful ventilation draws the air inward, maintaining the biosafety suite under negative pressure so a microbe can't drift upstream and escape.

The decomp area is like an air lock, a corridor with heavy doors at either end. On the right is an elevator to the garage, so a potentially infectious body can be moved directly from a vehicle into negative pressure without exposing the rest of the building.

Across from the body elevator is a walk-in refrigerator that contains about 125 unidentified bodies and body parts, some that have been kept for decades. Many are skeletal remains, some just a single bone. Nobody leaves the OCME unidentified. Efforts to learn names and bring families closure never end. The unknown are never forgotten.

Next to the refrigerator is the decomp freezer, where bodies in an advanced state of decomposition or infested with fly larvae are placed. Freezing slows decomposition. After a couple of days in the freezer, a body is solidified and the insects killed.

A second door, unlocked by a swipe card, leads to a corridor with three autopsy rooms. Each room has two stainless-steel autopsy stations beneath a low, brightly lit ceiling. Another door leads to a dressing room — where staff can don white Tyvek bunny suit protective gear — a shower and pass-through sterilizer, and an exit out of the biosafety suite.

The biosafety suite can operate independently of the rest of the OCME, with its own generator, ventilation, and plumbing. Even if the power goes out, even if the rest of Baltimore is incapacitated, the biosafety rooms will keep a deadly infectious agent contained. If necessary, the drains can be diverted into a hundred-thousand-gallon holding tank beneath the building for later decontamination. The entire suite can be sealed and sterilized with hydrogen peroxide vapor.

With six stations in the biosafety suite and eight in each main room, the OCME can comfortably conduct twenty-two autopsies at once. The OCME runs moderately but manageably busy with twelve to fourteen autopsies a day.

This was a different world, with its own strict rules and procedures. So much for me to learn when I first joined it.

I hadn't been at the OCME long when I received a call from an attorney in Pennsylvania. A child had died in the central part of that state and was being taken by hearse to a funeral home in

Hagerstown, Maryland. The attorney represented the child's paternal grandparents, who had concerns about the child's death. He asked the OCME to intercept the hearse and conduct a forensic investigation. Time was of the essence, because they were en route as we spoke.

Fowler wasn't in the office, and I didn't know what to do. I went down to the Investigations department, and an FI told me to see the on-call medical examiner. Everybody was downstairs in the autopsy suite attending morning rounds. I took the elevator down and walked to the wide accessing hallway outside of the two main autopsy rooms, where a group of autopsy techs was sitting.

The doors swung open into the voluminous, glaringly bright autopsy room. A cluster of two dozen or so doctors and students gathered around a gurney. All eyes turned to me as I asked for Dr. Patricia Aronica, who was on call for the day. They stepped aside as I relayed the urgent request to intercept a hearse.

Aronica gave me a look of vaguely annoyed disappointment, as though dealing with a toddler who'd spilled a bowl of soup on his lap. "We can't do that," she said. "We can only investigate deaths that occur in Maryland."

That . . . made sense. It's like golf: You play it as it lies. Each jurisdiction handles deaths that occur within its boundaries. If a person dies suddenly in Maryland, it's one of ours. If a person is shot in Maryland, taken to a hospital in Washington for treatment, and pronounced dead there, it's one of theirs. If you're driving from New York to Florida and die in a crash on I-95 in Maryland, or switching planes at BWI airport when you throw a clot and collapse in the terminal, you're one of ours.

So much to learn. I needed to study COMAR and the Annotated Code more.

Months into the job, I learned a harsh lesson when a twenty-nine-year-old woman from New York had a late-term abortion at a suburban Washington clinic. The fetus she was carrying had severe abnormalities. When the woman died days after the procedure, the OCME conducted the forensic investigation. The woman's death ignited a firestorm in the anti-abortion community.

She had died from disseminated intravascular coagulation due to amniotic fluid embolus. Basically, some of the amniotic fluid had leaked into the woman's bloodstream, a rare but known complication that can occur in pregnancy. The death was due to natural causes.

A reporter from an upstate New York newspaper called to get information on the woman's cause and manner of death. "What is disseminated intravascular coagulation?" he asked. I knew the answer. It's a disorder of uncontrolled clotting in the bloodstream and can exhaust the body's supply of clotting factor.

The reporter got it wrong, writing a story suggesting that the woman bled to death. I had inadvertently thrown gasoline on a raging fire. As soon as I saw the story appear online, I called the reporter and told him to correct the facts. But by then it was too late. His story had been picked up by news wires and was being repeated all over the internet.

The woman's parents were infuriated at the OCME, and rightly so. I felt terrible. To compound matters, it was Allan's case. I felt like such a failure, I could not bear to look her in the eye.

"I screwed up," I told Fowler. "I'll resign."

"Don't be ridiculous," he said, dialing the parents with his phone on speaker so I could hear.

I sat across from Fowler's desk and listened as the woman's parents spoke of the anguish the news stories caused. That I caused. My face burned with shame.

Fowler let the parents speak without interruption. He said that the reporter misquoted the OCME's spokesperson, and apologized for the unfortunate situation. "Most assuredly, we will do better going forward," he said, looking at me.

The experience made me realize that my job is not to be friendly or helpful to reporters. I work for the public. My duty is to the dead and protecting their interests. I failed in that case. But I resolved never to fail again. From now on, the answer to a question like that would be to Google it.

Thursday July 18, 2013, was a hot day, with the temperature spiking at 97 degrees Fahrenheit and still sweltering at 7:00 P.M. when Tyrone West drove his sister's 1999 Mercedes-Benz in a northeast Baltimore neighborhood.

He backed through an intersection and made a turn, an improper maneuver that I admit to having committed in the past.

West's driving caught the attention of Nicholas Chapman and Jorge Bernardez-Ruiz, members of Baltimore City Police Department's Northeast Operations Unit. The NOU was a special squad tasked with preventing violent crime and street drug dealing, a legacy of former mayor Martin O'Malley's zero-tolerance policing tactics.

The cops initiated a traffic stop. It was a pretextual stop, a minor matter that gives police an excuse to investigate further.

Ruiz told West to step out of the car and sit on the curb. Chapman began to search the driver's side of the car while Ruiz kept an eye on West, who was sitting on the curb with his legs extended. Ruiz told West to cross his legs, to reduce the risk of the officer tripping if he had to move suddenly. As West folded his legs, the cuff of his pants rose a few inches up his ankle, revealing a bulge in his sock and a peek of a clear plastic bag containing thirteen small glassine envelopes of cocaine.

It was an *oh shit* moment. West had been out of prison barely a year after serving twelve years for assault and drug distribution.

Another distribution charge would be very bad. West looked up at Ruiz, the cop's eyes fixed on the bulge in his sock.

Without a word spoken, the two men burst into action, grappling and throwing punches. At forty-four years of age, West was a substantial man who worked out often; his six-foot frame packed a solid 234 pounds.

As Ruiz and West struggled, Chapman called a Signal 13 over his radio. Signal 13 is an urgent call for immediate help. It means an officer faces an imminent threat, possibly a life-and-death situation, an emergency beacon to draw all available officers to the scene.

One of the cops deployed pepper spray, which managed to hit both of them while leaving West unaffected. The brawl continued with a flurry of punches and kicks. Chapman called a second Signal 13 and escalated the use of force, using a baton to hit West several times on the thigh to no effect. West escaped their grasp and ran across the street. Chapman called in a third Signal 13.

Fewer than four minutes had elapsed since Ruiz and Chapman stopped West's car, but it felt like a slow-motion eternity to the men scuffling in the stifling heat.

Within a minute of Chapman's third Signal 13, additional police arrived at the scene. Six officers swarmed onto West, pinning him prone on the ground. West was forced into submission and handcuffed with his arms behind his back. One officer knelt on West's back to keep him from getting up. Four more police officers pulled up as he was being restrained, bringing the number of cops at the scene to twelve.

At some point, one of the cops noticed that West was unresponsive and no longer breathing. Handcuffs were removed and West was rolled onto his back as an officer began CPR. An ambulance was summoned. EMTs initiated care and rushed West to Good Samaritan Hospital. Despite an aggressive resuscitation attempt in the emergency department, West was pronounced dead at 8:11 P.M.

During the autopsy the next day, assistant medical examiner Dr. Pamela Southall saw superficial scrapes and bruises on West's body that would be expected from a physical altercation on pavement. She also noted several linear marks on his lower back and thighs consistent with baton strikes. There were no signs of baton strikes or any other trauma to the head, neck, or face. No bone fractures anywhere on the body. All of the injuries involved the skin, subcutaneous layers, and fat. In a couple of spots, trauma extended slightly deeper into the muscle. None of these injuries, even considered together, are enough to kill a person.

Southall looked for signs of asphyxiation. She examined the horseshoe-shaped hyoid bone, found atop the larynx, and the slender strap muscles that hold the hyoid in place. Injury to these delicate structures can be a sign of choking or strangulation. No injuries were seen on West's hyoid or strap muscles. She looked for petechiae, pinpoint ruptures in capillary beds that can be caused by asphyxia. Nothing.

The absence of evidence, the saying goes, is not evidence of absence. The lack of signs is not evidence that West was uninjured. A choke hold can kill within seconds. Where was that knee — on the lower back, or up by the shoulder near his neck? Southall was unable to ask the cops whether anybody compressed West's neck with a forearm or knee because they declined to cooperate with her investigation. It could not be ruled out.

Lab tests indicated that West was dehydrated at the time of his death. He also had cocaine metabolites in his urine, but none of the drug — or any other drug — was detected in his bloodstream.

Examination of thin sections of heart tissue by a cardiac pathologist revealed abnormal tissue in the left bundle branch and Purkinje fibers, the circuit that conducts the electrical impulse from the heart's pacemaker to the lower chambers.

The last page of a postmortem examination report is the opin-ion section, in which the medical examiner distills facts into a concise conclusion. Opinions are typically a few sentences of clinical terms, a brief paragraph. Southall's thoughtfully written opinion speaks directly to the West family and, by extension, the public at large. She purposefully used clear lay language to explain her interpretation of the facts.

> The abnormalities found in Mr. West's heart and signs of dehydration are certainly causes for sudden cardiac death. Another factor that may have contributed to his death was extreme environmental temperature . . . The cardiac conduction system abnormality is a predisposing factor for cardiac arrhythmia because the conduction system controls the heart rate by generating and conduct-ing electrical impulses throughout the heart muscle, causing the heart to contract and pump blood through-out the body. Defects in the system can predispose one to sudden death. One way dehydration stresses the body is by causing the heart to beat harder and irregularly, caus-ing a fatal heart rhythm and sudden death. Extreme heat can stress the body in many ways, one being an increase in heart rate. These were all predisposing factors for sudden death in the case of Mr. West. The investigation showed that Mr. West fought with several police officers and resisted restraint for several minutes prior to becom-ing suddenly and unexpectedly unresponsive. This period was likely associated with a high output of adrenaline, leading to increased energy exertion and use of oxygen reserves that further increased the stress on his heart. To conclude, in the absence of significant injury and signs of asphyxia, all of the prevailing factors in this case increased his potential for sudden death.

On the death certificate, Southall identified West's cause of death as cardiac arrhythmia and "cardiac conduction system abnormality complicated by dehydration during police restraint."

Manner of death is a categorization based on how the death occurred. The National Association of Medical Examiners publishes a guide to classify manner of death, aptly titled "A Guide for Manner of Death Classification." The principles in the NAME classification guide are followed by the OCME and all accredited medical examiner offices.

Deaths due to natural causes are exclusively the result of a disease or biological process, with no other non-natural factor such as a fall or other injury. West had an underlying medical condition, but his engagement with the police is a non-natural factor. Natural causes was out as West's manner of death, as was suicide for obvious reasons.

That left accident and homicide. If the exertion of his struggle with the police — adrenaline coursing through his system, blood pressure rising and heart pounding, at the peak of his fight-or-flight response — triggered an arrhythmia, the manner of death is accident. A homicide is a death at the hands of another person. If West died because an officer pressed on his neck, that would be a homicide.

Medical examiners must be sure about their cause and manner of death determinations. Maryland statute demands that the medical examiner's determinations be within "a reasonable degree of medical certainty." The NAME classification guide uses similar language, specifying that evidence for the cause and manner of death be "compelling." Medical examiners can't assume or speculate, or rely upon possibilities or probabilities. The determination is a certainty, or it isn't. There is no gray area.

Without evidence to the contrary, Southall couldn't be certain that something untoward didn't happen to West while being restrained.

Two forces clashed that summer evening on Kitmore Road: Tyrone West, with his predisposition for arrhythmia and sudden death, and the police. Which one was more responsible for his death? Southall couldn't say for sure.

When a case is on the bubble like that, when the evidence for one manner of death is equal to one or more other manners of death, a toss-up between accident and homicide in this case, the NAME guideline categorizes the manner of death as undetermined. Such are the limits of forensic medicine.

"What could not be determined from forensic investigation and autopsy findings was the absolute relative contribution of each factor in causing his death. Therefore, the manner of death is COULD NOT BE DETERMINED," she concluded in her report.

In the fall of 2013, a news story was brought to the attention of Rebecca Jufer Phipps, PhD, chief of the OCME's toxicology laboratory — the first lab accredited by the American Board of Forensic Toxicology; a certificate with the serial number 0001 hangs on the wall of a large room with rows of analytical instruments. Angular white scoops resembling robotic arms descend from the ceiling to vent heat produced by the machines. Jufer Phipps trained under Barry Levine, head of the lab for twenty years and author of *Principles of Forensic Toxicology*, widely used by universities and colleges as a textbook and considered an essential reference on the subject.

The brief news story reported on an unusual cluster of twenty-three fentanyl deaths in Ohio during the month of November. Fentanyl is a synthetic opioid used to treat severe pain, such as to ease the discomfort of cancer, often as a patch that slowly administers the drug through the skin. The drug is up to fifty times stronger than heroin and one hundred times stronger than morphine. The OCME occasionally has cases in which people used multiple fentanyl patches, chewed them to extract the drug, or even tried smoking the plastic patches. Now people were dying from the drug in its pure form.

Piqued by the news account, Jufer Phipps ran a search of lab results and was alarmed to discover thirty-seven fentanyl deaths in Maryland during the past three months. Fentanyl had come to the OCME.

— CHAPTER FOUR —

SMALLTIMORE

Mornings begin with a review of the daily conference sheet, the list of those at the OCME for autopsy, to get a sense of how busy things will be and whether any cases are likely to attract media attention.

Subject found deceased, drug paraphernalia present . . . Subject discovered unresponsive on toilet; paramedics are concerned he choked on food . . . Subject was the driver of a Jeep that hit a tow truck that was sliding out of control . . . Subject with history of drug use found deceased at residence . . . Subject was a passenger who was ejected . . . Subject was found hanging in a secure residence . . . Unidentified adult discovered on sidewalk with multiple gunshot wounds . . .

The conference sheet is a litany of bad decisions and unfortunate circumstances.

One morning I was browsing the daily conference sheet and recognized a familiar name, a prominent writer in Baltimore's literary scene. That's Smalltimore. A gifted writer, this woman had studied creative writing at Johns Hopkins and was the recipient of fellowships and awards. The real deal. I had met her a few years earlier, when we were among those doing readings at a literary event. She was very generous with her time and talent, one of those people everybody seems to know and love.

She lived in a row house that had been divided into apartments, as many are in Baltimore. Neighbors complained about an unpleasant odor in the building. She was found dead in her apartment, locked from the inside. No signs of foul play. Her death turned out to be due to natural causes.

She was last seen alive three weeks earlier. Missing in action for twenty-one days, including over her birthday. Dozens of friends wrote on her Facebook page wishing her birthday greetings. Three days later, she was found dead.

There was an outpouring of tributes and praise in her memory. Friends posted tearful messages on Facebook. Within days, one mutual friend published a lovely remembrance in a local online publication. It was all very touching.

But I wondered. Where was everybody during those three weeks? She had no lunches, no dates, no appointments, no place where she was expected, no deadlines, nobody she hung out with? How long could I be missing before somebody became concerned?

Everybody, including me, thought this woman was socially integral. A friend to everybody. But during those three weeks she had nobody. The thought filled me with sadness. I felt an urge to say something on her behalf. But due to the constraints of my job, I couldn't.

Being on the receiving end of phone calls from reporters was an eye-opening experience. Reading the news online, I'd mutter under my breath at stories that got facts wrong about the OCME or an investigation. "Let it go," Fowler advised me. "It doesn't matter what people say. We'll still be in business tomorrow. Our budget doesn't get bigger if people like us. It doesn't make a difference one way or another."

In its seventy-four years of existence, the OCME has never requested a correction to a news story, never written a letter to the editor, never issued a press release. It's an agency that doesn't care what people think. I have the strangest PR job ever.

From the outside, the OCME is an impenetrable black box. During my time as a reporter, I had firsthand experience trying to get information from the medical examiner office for a news story about a shooting, car crash, or fatal house fire. Even getting basic facts like the number of victims, their sex and age, was impossible until a police or fire official eventually got around to releasing the information.

As a journalist I took pride in my craft. I enjoyed piecing together facts into a news story, reaching for vivid details to make it interesting reading. My story for *Patch* about the brutal 2011 hatchet killing of eighteen-year-old Ryan Jackson earned praise from colleagues. Like many homicides, Jackson's death was the result of an impulsive burst of rage, with little forethought or planning. His killer, Larry Horton, did little to conceal evidence, tossing the murder weapon in the trash can by his kitchen door. He's serving life in prison now.

I went to the crime scene for my *Patch* story, interviewed Jackson's girlfriend, pregnant with his child, and his family. I described the blood splattered on the walls and ceiling, the outline of a body on a blood-soaked couch. After gaining on-the-job experience in my role at the OCME and access to confidential information, though, I questioned how readers were served by my account of Jackson's murder. Were they better informed? I'm not so sure. Jackson's case file at the OCME told a different story, one more horrific than I'd been able to tell through my reporting.

The experience with Ryan Jackson's homicide helped me to understand why information about deaths was so difficult to acquire from the OCME. The body, the autopsy report, and all the work done within the OCME are evidence. In the American criminal justice system, Fowler lectured me, evidence is kept confidential. A courtroom is the venue for examining and discussing evidence. The public doesn't have the right to see accounting records, for instance, when somebody is charged with fraud. That isn't how it works.

Premature release of information could advantage one side or another, give accused assailants a sneak peek at the evidence against them, provide an opportunity for witnesses to change their stories or be tampered with. It could lead to a mistrial. Guarding the confidentiality of information is as essential for the integrity of an investigation as maintaining a chain of custody.

No information about a case is released while the investigation is ongoing. Ever. Until a case is concluded and the cause and manner of death determined, any case could potentially be a criminal matter. The rule about releasing information applies to any investigation by any agency — police, arson investigation, a state's attorney's office, the Occupational Safety and Health Administration, the National Transportation Safety Board, and so on.

Working at the OCME is a privilege and a curse for a reformed reporter. When a major incident happens, police set up two perimeters around the scene. The public is kept at a far distance, maybe blocks away. The only people allowed within the perimeter are police, fire, and EMS personnel. There is a second, inner perimeter around the active scene that is off-limits to all except detectives and crime scene technicians who need to be there.

As a reporter, I've covered countless shootings, fires, crashes and other incidents, trying to glean details for my story. Reporters are often allowed within the outer perimeter, closer than the public, but they are kept well away from the active scene. The press, and in turn the public, does not have much of an idea of what actually happened until information is released by the police.

Now that I am part of the OCME, I'm not just within the inner perimeter, I have access to information that nobody else has.

Crime scene photos. Police reports. Investigator reports. A murder-suicide makes the news. A fatal multiple-vehicle crash tied up the morning rush-hour traffic. Facebook is abuzz about a body found floating in the Inner Harbor. I know who they are, details of their background, and what happened. I know what their tattoos look like, what they carried in their pockets. People read about a child tragically killed. The child's mother calls me for information. The conference sheet often lists decedents killed in particularly disturbing or heinous circumstances, victims of shocking crimes that never make the news. Based on my reporting sense, people would want to know about these incidents. My reflexes are to inform the public. But I can't tell anybody. I'm cursed with knowing stories that can't be told.

I learned to pay careful attention to what I said, where, and to whom. Years ago, two medical examiners had drinks at the restaurant across from the Penn Street building after work and talked about one of their cases, a shooting death. Just shop talk between colleagues. After a while, a guy who was sitting behind them at a table came over and said, "I'm an attorney and heard every word. You should know better than talking about that in public."

Another doctor told me about the time he was dealing with the brother of a homicide victim and spoke with him several times on the phone about his sister's fatal injuries, only to learn while testifying on the witness stand that the brother was also the accused killer. That kind of complication can throw a wrench into a prosecution.

The less said the better. You can't go wrong keeping your mouth shut. Never talk about work with friends and family, I learned. Especially friends, because that leads to friends of friends. Due to the Smalltimore effect, it won't take long to reach the family of the victim, followed by an angry phone call to the governor's office. Leaking information can land an employee of an investigative agency in hot water.

"Did you guys get that shooting in Pigtown yesterday?" my buddy Dale Thieler asked.

"If it happened in Maryland, the OCME is involved," I said.

"You don't say much about work," he said.

"Yup. I like my job," I replied.

"What's the worst thing you've seen?"

"Your mom."

As time permitted, I read and re-read the Maryland Annotated Code and COMAR — the guide rails defining the OCME's authority and operation — and the Maryland Public Information Act, which covers the release of documents and records.

According to the law, Fowler is an employee of the Postmortem Examiners Commission, although he is paid by the Department of Health. No individual in the state can fire the chief medical examiner. Not the secretary of health, not the governor. It takes a majority of the five-member commission to fire, or hire, a chief and his assistant medical examiners and key staff of the OCME.

"The Commission may employ a staff in accordance with the State budget for the operation of the Commission and to maintain accreditation," the law says.

I brushed up on reporting deaths, criteria for cases the medical examiner must investigate, the transportation of bodies for examination, the requirements for autopsy reports, and the right of family or guardians to appeal cause and manner of death rulings. I also learned about the disposition of unclaimed bodies, donation of bodies for medical education through the State Anatomy Board, and other intricacies related to death.

I was surprised by what is not in the law. A person doesn't have to be next of kin or even related to a decedent to claim a body. The OCME releases bodies to any funeral home with a signed authorization. Anyone can make arrangements with a funeral home for an unclaimed body. Sometimes a friend, a group of co-workers, or a church congregation steps up to make sure an unclaimed decedent has a proper funeral.

On occasion, families are in conflict over the disposition of a body. One sibling wants a direct cremation while another wants a memorial service with an open casket. The OCME doesn't get in the middle of family disputes. The first to make arrangements with a funeral home wins. Let them fight it out among themselves. Once a body has been examined and leaves the building, it is not the OCME's concern anymore.

Own a roomy SUV? No law or regulation requires a body to be picked up by a funeral home or transported in a hearse or specialized vehicle. A person can legally use their own vehicle to transport a body for cremation or burial. Strapping the body to a roof rack is ill advised.

I thought of Bocce Club Pizza, my family's favorite pizza place growing up in Amherst. You could drop by anytime and buy an unclaimed pizza that somebody ordered but didn't pick up. If a person is hungry and open to random pizza toppings, it's a good deal.

The implications of the law were alarming. "If I'm reading this correctly," I said to Fowler, "a person could drop by the OCME and claim a random unclaimed body, put it in the back of their Subaru, and drive off."

"Nothing in the law prohibits it," he said.

On very rare occasions, a body is removed from the OCME in a privately owned vehicle. Once in a while a person chooses a "green" burial, unembalmed and wrapped in a cloth shroud. A body can be buried on private property with few restrictions. In these cases, the family or death doula acts as the funeral director and must follow the laws and fulfill the requirements for interment and completing the death certificate.

"They have to come back and show me the completed death certificate," Donnell McCullough, the autopsy department supervisor, told me. "I have to know where that decedent is buried. We don't want the body dumped at the side of a road somewhere and come back as another case."

Nothing in the law prohibits a person from keeping a dead body in a private home, as long as the neighbors don't complain. That's literally what the Annotated Code says:

> A health officer may take control of a body that is being kept in a room where an individual lives and that is in a condition that endangers an individual in the house where the body is kept if:
> At least 3 individuals living near the house or a physician asks the health officer, in writing, to order final disposition of the body . . .

Loopholes in the law allow for some unanticipated situations. While first responders and health professionals are required by law to report deaths to the police, that duty does not apply to the general public. No law requires a private citizen to report a death.

In the late 1990s, an Arundel County man buried his three-year-old daughter in a wooded area near his home when she died unexpectedly in his care. The girl was reported missing by her non-custodial mother, living out of state, who hadn't seen or heard from her daughter in months, including a missed visitation that had been scheduled for the Christmas holiday. She reported her daughter missing the next summer, eight months after her death. The father said that he panicked when the toddler died. He buried her body and never informed the mother. As strange and heartbreaking as it all is, not a single law was broken. The child had a seizure disorder and died of natural causes. No foul play was involved. Her father wasn't required to report her death to any authorities, and he buried her on private property.

"There's nothing that says you can't bury your husband, wife, or child in the backyard, as morbid as that sounds," a state's attorney's office spokesperson told a reporter.

I listened to a podcast of the Stoop Storytelling series, a Baltimore event at which true stories are told in front of a live audience with no notes. It's an enjoyable event in which I've had the opportunity to perform a couple of times. The podcast episode featured stories with the theme of "crime, punishment, and life (and death) in the legal system," and one of the storytellers was a man named Stephen Janis.

I knew Janis. We had met for coffee once during my days as a reporter to talk about the separate websites we were trying to develop and the potential for partnering on advertising sales. He was an active freelancer like me, writing for the alternative weekly *Baltimore City Paper*, *The Baltimore Examiner*, and other media around town. At the time, Janis ran the news site Investigative Voice, and I had a side project that I noodled with, a sort of city guide called Welcome to Baltimore, Hon. Neither of us had enough traffic to be commercially viable.

"People in Baltimore die in a lot of very spectacularly violent and horrifying ways," he began in his Stoop story. "It's our job as reporters to cover it."

Janis said that *The Examiner* covered every protest in Baltimore. Conflict always makes for a good story. "If there were two people, it was a protest because we had to write two stories a day," he said. "I even got good at taking pictures at odd angles to make it look like there were more people there." That was his laugh line.

He talked about covering a protest in lower Park Heights, a neighborhood in northwest Baltimore, in 2006. A group of people believed a serial killer was preying on women in their community, responsible for as many as seven to fifteen victims.

Police said that their concerns were unfounded. The protest was to draw attention to Tyra McClary, a thirty-six-year-old woman who died in August of that year. She had been found decomposed, partially covered with mulch, with her feet in a garbage bag. The medical examiner determined that her death was due to intoxication of morphine, methadone, and cocaine. The manner of death was undetermined.

"That means the medical examiner can't rule homicide, suicide, natural, or accident, so these deaths end up in limbo," Janis said.

Janis claimed that McClary's body had signs of asphyxiation, a conclusion not supported by her autopsy report. He suggested that she may have been one of many women strangled by an unknown serial killer lurking in lower Park Heights. As many as twenty-nine women whose drug-related deaths were ruled undetermined may have been victims.

He wrote a story for *The Examiner* that he admitted was "not subtle" about the serial killer angle. "People took exception to that characterization," Janis said. "My story became contentious."

Nonetheless, he insists that he was right and that suggesting a serial killer was likely responsible for what appears to have been another tragic drug intoxication was the right thing to do.

"By not telling the stories of the dead, we do a disservice to the community," Janis said in concluding his Stoop story. "Telling their stories is one of the most noble occupations a person can do."

That's quite a story — the intrepid journalist heroically tracking a serial killer who victimized drug users, sex workers, and other vulnerable women. If only there was any evidence it were true.

"The Nose," an un-bylined media critic column that ran in *City Paper*, called Janis out on his serial killer theory.

Worse than Baltimore's usual horrific murder total, these young girls were bound and slashed — in some cases beheaded — according to a neighborhood barber. And the police are actively covering it up.

What a story.

Good thing it's total crap. How does the Nose know?

Because there are no slashed, dead bodies. There are no outraged relatives of missing girls. There is, in fact, no evidence at all to indicate even a single woman was killed in that neighborhood over the past several months. The one victim . . . Tyra McClary, died of a drug overdose in late August. Her head was not cut off . . . She was not found half-buried . . .

The Examiner's persistence in the face of no evidence has frustrated police.

"I'm not sure what their agenda is," Baltimore City Police Department spokesman Matt Jablow says. "It's amazing to me that this still has legs. This is the Loch Ness monster."

The undetermined manner of death designation is often applied to drug intoxications. Although the OCME's motto is "Search for Truth," there are limits to what is knowable. Was the drug more powerful than the deceased expected? Maybe they thought it was heroin, unaware that it contained fentanyl. That would be an accident. Did somebody administer the drug, inject them with a lethal dose? In that case the manner of death is homicide. Was it an intentional act to end their life? Suicides are often spontaneous, done on the spur of the moment. It's impossible to know somebody's state of mind, to infer their intent. So when the facts don't support a conclusion to a degree of certainty, the manner of death is ruled undetermined.

"It may not be satisfactory to everybody," Fowler explained to me, "but it is intellectually honest."

The Maryland OCME is criticized for categorizing drug intoxication deaths as undetermined. Some of these cases, the argument goes, are accidents, suicides, and homicides. The statistical data may not be accurate, they say. Other jurisdictions rule the manner of these deaths as accidental. This approach risks missing cases that may actually be suicides or homicides. Statistics based on this definition are no more accurate than the OCME's. There is no perfect solution. Maryland is an outlier for undetermined manner of death. That's the way it's done. Perhaps not perfect, but consistent and honest.

"I can't help it if everybody else is doing it wrong," joked Jerry D., the OCME's retired administrator, who still works part-time at the agency.

Bodies get dumped in Baltimore all the time. Leakin Park, a densely wooded secluded area in West Baltimore, is so notorious as a dumping ground that people keep track of them on blogs and Google Maps. Few of the dead dumped in Baltimore are victims of homicide.

I read the forensic investigator's report of one case that came into the OCME in which a group of people were partying with heroin and cocaine in my old Union Square neighborhood. One member of the group overdosed and died. His buddies carried his body out the back door and deposited him under the steps of a row house up the block, then went back to continue the festivities.

It happens. People do all sorts of undignified and disrespectful things. A body turns up inconveniently dead and somebody says, "Get 'em out of here. I don't want this in my house." So the body gets rolled up in a blanket or stuffed in a trash bag and tossed somewhere.

Things can look awful. Clothing can get disheveled or pulled down when a body is dragged, making it look like a person was sexually assaulted. Spots of discoloration develop on the skin that can look like bruises from a beating. Blood will naturally trickle from the nose and mouth. Things frequently aren't as they appear.

At a homicide seminar session on bloodstain analysis at the OCME, the presenter showed a photo of a scene where a woman in her sixties was dead on the floor of her kitchen. Her body and the entire image was a bloody nightmare — droplets and splatters of blood, smears on the cabinets and floor, bloody footprints and handprints, and her bloody body lying in a pool of blood, her top pulled up and panties down her thighs. It looked like this poor woman was sexually assaulted and slaughtered.

However, the woman's residence was secure, locked from the inside with no sign of forced entry. There were no signs of a struggle, nothing disturbed or out of place. The woman was an alcoholic, intoxicated when she hit her head and caused a small laceration on her scalp, an inch or so long. Normally, a cut like this wouldn't be serious and would be unlikely to result in death. But chronic alcoholism damages the liver, which produces blood-clotting factors. The bleeding wouldn't stop, and in her inebriated state she walked around rather than phoning for help. She tried to clean up the mess while continuing to bleed uncontrollably until she went into shock and died. The footprints and handprints were hers; the smears, traces of her attempts to mop up the blood. People in the throes of moribund shock do irrational things as they lose their grasp on consciousness, thrashing and pulling at clothing. For people suffering from hypothermia, this behavior is known as paradoxical undressing.

Things aren't always as they appear, which is why sudden and unexpected deaths deserve a patient, thorough investigation by qualified professionals.

At the OCME, cases are presented at morning rounds, where the medical examiners, students, and others in attendance learn about and observe the body. Then, when the autopsies have been completed for the day, the results are presented at an afternoon conference where cases are discussed among the group. Medical examiners make their cause and manner of death determinations with a reasonable degree of medical certainty. No guesses or presumptions are allowed.

The chief reviews all cases for which the manner of death is undetermined, as he does with all homicides and deaths of babies and children, to make sure that the investigation was done properly and nothing was overlooked. This quality-control process — peer review and supervisory review — provides assurance that the conclusions are the best fit for the facts.

I ignored Fowler's advice about dealing with the press and emailed Janis. I told him that his story about McClary was inaccurate and needlessly alarming. In particular, the use of *limbo* bothered me. He'd made it sound like these people are abandoned, as though nobody cares. My exchange with him resolved nothing, but I was glad I called him on it nonetheless.

The United States has a patchwork of more than two thousand different death investigation systems. Some are jurisdictions overseen by coroners, some by medical examiners, and some are a mixture of both. Forensic autopsies — for the purpose of determining the cause and manner of death — are regularly performed at only seventy-four places throughout the country. Everywhere else, examinations are done at a hospital or funeral home, an independently operated morgue, or some guy's garage. Or not at all.

Of the seventy-four forensic medical centers in the United States, only fifty-five are fully accredited by the National Association of Medical Examiners. More than an ornamental ribbon, accreditation is an endorsement of competence. It is a rigorous peer-reviewed process that ensures a medical examiner is equipped for the proper practice of forensic medicine, and the organization well serves its jurisdiction. Where the Annotated Code and COMAR define the outlines of the OCME's operation, accreditation governs a multitude of day-to-day activities.

NAME accreditation is essential to an OCME's integrity. An unaccredited university is considered second-rate; similarly, the NAME endorsement is key to an organization's credibility. Without accreditation, there is no training program. Courts have less confidence in forensic evidence and the testimony of medical examiners.

The accreditation process involves a site visit and inspection by a team of reviewers from other accredited medical examiner offices. The team completes a 353-item checklist covering everything from investigations and autopsies to record keeping. Many of the items on the NAME accreditation checklist are non-specific performance standards, such as whether office space provided for doctors is "adequate for their work," without defining *adequate* or a certain number of square feet of space. It's a subjective opinion.

Relatively minor issues that don't directly affect the quality of work or the safety of personnel or the public are called Phase I deficiencies. Phase II deficiencies are more serious. These violations of standards may seriously affect the quality of work or pose a risk to the public or staff. To have full accreditation, an office is allowed up to fifteen Phase I deficiencies but can have no Phase II violations.

Failing to perform an autopsy within forty-eight hours of taking custody of a body in at least 90 percent of the cases is a

Phase I deficiency. That's bad. Not doing an autopsy within seventy-three hours in at least 90 percent of the cases is a Phase II violation. That's very bad. Some medical examiner and coroner offices hold bodies for several days before autopsies are performed. That's awful.

At the OCME, autopsies are completed within twenty-four hours more than 99 percent of the time. Not just homicides, but all of them.

One important metric is the number of autopsies performed by medical examiners each year. The NAME accreditation standard limits the number of autopsies a medical examiner should perform in a year. Experience has shown that thoroughness and proficiency drop off when a medical examiner has a high caseload. Too many autopsies, and there is a tendency to rush things along. Corners may get cut. Evidence may be overlooked. A high caseload also leaves less surge capacity in the event of a multiple-fatality incident. Autopsy reports take longer to produce, which can stall criminal investigations and delay getting much-needed death benefits into the hands of families.

The reasonable limit of cases per medical examiner per year is 250. Exceeding that limit is a Phase I deficiency. Having medical examiners perform more than 325 autopsies annually is far more serious, a Phase II deficiency.

The OCME has an unbroken thirty-five-year record of NAME accreditation. The last NAME inspection of the OCME prior to 2014 was in 2008, at the Penn Street building. Due to the poor condition of the facility, the agency was put on provisional accreditation status, giving it the opportunity to correct violations. Because the West Baltimore Street building was under construction at the time, which showed a good-faith effort to remedy deficiencies, the OCME was allowed to skate on provisional accreditation.

In 2014, the OCME was scheduled for its first NAME accreditation site visit in its new building. For the most part, the office was in pretty good shape.

One minor item in the NAME accreditation checklist was related to building safety: *Are building evacuation diagrams available and posted in appropriate locations throughout the facility?* The OCME didn't have fire escape diagrams posted in the building, which violated not only NAME standards but also local fire code.

Fire escape diagrams are one of those things people rarely have to think about, the kind of task that can get overlooked when setting up shop in a new building. Where do you buy fire escape route diagrams? Who do you hire? The OCME's maintenance chief made a few calls and got bids in the thousands of dollars.

We had the blueprints for the building as high-resolution .jpg images. I opened the blueprints in Photoshop and erased all of the notations and symbols, leaving just the walls, doorways, and stairwells of each floor. Then I highlighted the stairwells and exits in red and added arrows to show the evacuation route. Each floor needed four to six individualized diagrams, which were printed in color and mounted by the maintenance department in cheap certificate frames.

A few hours of my time was all it took to bring the OCME into compliance with the fire code and the NAME accreditation checklist. The evacuation route diagrams still give me a sense of satisfaction when I see them throughout the workday, reminders of my first tangible, permanent contribution to the organization.

The OCME aced the accreditation site inspection with three Phase I and zero Phase II deficiencies. A couple of the violations for which the OCME was cited can't be fixed. NAME accreditation requires that all forensic investigators be certified by the

American Board of Medicolegal Death Investigators. Some of the senior FIs have been at the OCME for decades, since before ABMDI existed, and if they don't want to bother taking the test that's their choice. State law prohibits forcing a state employee to meet a new requirement to keep their present job.

The other Phase I deficiency that would go unremedied was that one of the staff medical examiners was not board certified, as required for NAME accreditation. He took the medical boards twice, failed each time, and gave up. He's widely regarded as one of the best clinicians and teachers at the OCME. But he doesn't test well. Not a big deal.

Autopsy caseload, the third Phase I violation, was another matter. After fluctuating around ten thousand investigations, give or take a few hundred, for several years, the number of investigations rose to 10,751 cases in 2013 and was continuing to trend upward. An increase of about 700 autopsy cases, spread across the medical examiner staff, raised the average autopsies to 280 per doctor per year, a situation that had to be remedied.

All in all, pretty good. With three dings out of the 353-item accreditation checklist, the OCME was more than 99 percent compliant.

The troubling autopsy caseload statistics, however, obscured a more concerning truth. Autopsies were not evenly distributed. Not every medical examiner carried a full caseload. The two deputy chiefs handled cases only half-time, with the remainder spent on supervising autopsy operations, labs, and investigations. The chief didn't do any autopsies, so as to preserve a hierarchy of supervision and review. But they counted as examiners when averaging cases per person, as did the three fellows and one part-time medical examiner. In reality, ten of the thirteen staff medical examiners were exceeding 325 autopsies per year, and one was doing more than 400.

To stave off having the caseload average blow up into a Phase II violation, Fowler began the bureaucratic process of hiring another medical examiner. One more forensic pathologist would bring the average down to where it needed to be for the sake of compliance and best practices.

Walking through the OCME parking garage, I encountered Ricardo Diggs, one of the autopsy techs. Diggs prefers to work in the biosafety suite, the rooms under negative pressure where infectious and decomposed bodies are examined — he calls himself the Ambassador of Decomp — but works in the main autopsy rooms as well. A large, bearded man with glasses that make his eyes look owlish, Diggs is a former marine who served as a sniper in the Gulf War.

"I just don't know about people," he said.

"What's up, Ricardo?" I asked.

"We have a guy this morning who died on a Megabus on the Washington Beltway," he said. "I eviscerated him, and he had two ounces of crack cocaine in his rectum, wrapped up in a condom."

"On a bus?"

"Yeah," he said, forming his fingers to outline a shape the size of a sausage bun. "Two ounces. The condom broke."

"But why . . ."

"I know, right?"

"There's no security to pass to ride on a bus. He could have carried it in a backpack."

"Two ounces," Diggs repeated, contemplating the volume between his hands. "Gotta be uncomfortable sitting on a bus."

"Even if he flew in from someplace and transferred to a bus, it doesn't make sense," I said. "If that were me, I'd head for the bathroom as soon as I got through the terminal."

"Well, he failed at bodypacking," Diggs said. "He won't make that mistake again."

I went to Fowler and told him I wanted to poke some holes through the black box, let some public light penetrate the shroud around the OCME. "There is value to banking goodwill with the public," I said. In the absence of information, people will think the worst. We can do more to explain what the OCME is and how it works. The OCME is an example of government doing something right. I felt that Marylanders should understand and appreciate how their taxes were being spent.

He asked me, what was the upside potential and what was the downside risk? That was his calculus when considering new ideas. "I like to stay below the radar," he said. No social media. Facebook and Instagram were out of the question, and any Twitter announcements would continue to come from the Department of Health's account.

Some medical examiner offices have gift shops selling T-shirts and merch. Maryland's OCME has nothing like that. I was given an OCME jacket with the rest of the staff, but nothing is available to the public. The only item of swag at the OCME is a commemorative challenge coin. One side featured the OCME's seal. The reverse had artwork of the sculpture that used to hang by the entrance of the Penn Street building and the motto "Search for Truth." Prized by many as collectible items, the challenge coins are given only by the chief at his discretion. Fowler gave me one as a holiday present my first year on the job.

I wasn't the first to ask Fowler about opening an OCME gift shop. He said it wasn't a good idea to have cash floating around the building. As for selling items such as a T-shirt with a body outline in a city with a homicide history like Baltimore's, that would be of questionable taste. Too much downside risk.

"The OCME is authorized by law to investigate deaths that occur in Maryland," he told me. "That's all we do. As long as you stay within the law, you are protected. When you do other things, you can wander into trouble and invite criticism."

Bringing media inside the OCME is always a dicey proposition. All of the medical examiners on staff had been burned by reporters at one time or another, misquoted or made to look incompetent or corrupt. As a result, most are quite hostile toward the media, and none of them, except for Fowler, would ever speak with reporters or comment on cases. Everything there is to be said about an investigation is in the autopsy report.

The OCME medical examiners don't like having their faces appear in photos or news video. Parents and grandparents have been charged with abuse of children, families torn apart, because of their testimony. Dangerously violent gang members have been put behind bars for life based on their work.

Fowler refuses to appear on cable news or true-crime shows. He had one bad experience on *Nancy Grace*, the former prosecutor's program that aired for several years on CNN's Headline News channel. "You sit in a little booth," he told me. "There's no monitor, so you're talking to yourself, and you have a few seconds to give some sound bites. It was a waste of time. I'll never do something like that again."

Before my time at the OCME, Fowler had made one exception to his true-crime aversion. He sat for an interview for an episode of the *Forensic Files* TV show titled "Whodunit," which aired on August 6, 2001. The program was about the 1998 murder of Stephen Hricko by his wife, Kimberly. The real-life details of the Hricko murder sound like the plot summary of a television drama. During a romantic Valentine's Day getaway at a waterfront resort, the Hrickos enjoyed a murder mystery dinner performance, sharing a table with a state's attorney and her husband. Afterward, Kimberly Hricko, a surgical technician, allegedly killed her husband with a fatal dose of succinylcholine, a rapidly acting paralytic drug that stops the breathing and can be undetectable within minutes. She scattered empty beer bottles and set fire to the bed, staging the scene to look as though her husband was intoxicated and smoking in bed, and then she went for a drive. When she returned, the room was on fire and she summoned help.

Fowler's examination of Stephen Hricko's body revealed no soot in his airway and no carboxyhemoglobin — formed when blood is exposed to carbon monoxide — in his bloodstream. He was dead before the fire started. Toxicology found no alcohol in his blood, so he hadn't been drinking. Fowler could not find any other injuries, serious cardiovascular disease, or any other cause of death.

Kimberly Hricko was convicted of first-degree murder and is serving life in prison plus thirty years.

Every few months I'd get an inquiry from a video production company interested in basing a reality show at the OCME. I didn't even have to ask Fowler. I already knew the answer would be no. Nobody wants a camera following them around.

The chief had me assume his duties hosting and presenting to grand juries that tour the OCME. The courts arrange tours for grand jurors, both to inform them about law enforcement and forensic investigation and also to break up the monotony of sitting in the grand jury room for three months. Grand juries visit the OCME, the police crime lab and shooting range, and the Central Processing unit of the city jail. After having me sit through one of his PowerPoint presentations about the OCME, he said I would do them from then on.

In addition to grand juries, I handled requests for tours from forensic science and criminal justice classes from area universities, interns from state's attorney's offices and circuit court clerks, and other groups.

Following considerable negotiation of the ground rules, Fowler allowed me to bring a *Baltimore Sun* reporter and photographer into the building for a summer photo series called "Hidden Maryland," about places that the public doesn't usually get to see. It was an opportunity to showcase the new building. There were strict restrictions — no bodies, no body bags, no tissue, no case numbers or any identifiable information, and no evidence. Given there is evidence throughout the building — on desks and in offices, on photocopiers, et cetera, and the two journalists would not even necessarily know what was and was not evidence, I had to stick by them, reporter Justin George and photographer Lloyd Fox, and make sure nothing was surreptitiously recorded. Every photo Fox took was reviewed.

Fox's photo essay and George's twelve-hundred-word text constituted the first time the OCME had opened up like that. Now that I'd gained Fowler's trust, he allowed me to host reporters, photographers, filmmakers and videographers, and podcasters. I was pleased to make the agency more transparent and less of an impenetrable, unknown entity.

In October 2014, I began listening to the *Serial* podcast about the 1999 murder of Hae Min Lee. The case was particularly unsettling because it happened close to home. Many of the landmarks the podcast mentioned were familiar places in my neighborhood: Woodlawn High School and the public library across the street, Leakin Park, the Best Buy on Security Boulevard, Patapsco State Park.

Serial was hugely popular, and chatter about the case against Adnan Syed was all over Facebook and Reddit, with amateur sleuths debating the significance of developments the latest episode revealed. Supporters convinced of Syed's innocence hoped to get his conviction reconsidered.

I was worried that Hae Min Lee's case file could become a target for amateur investigators and souvenir seekers. We didn't need documents or photos appearing on the internet. I asked OCME's records department to have Hae Min Lee's case file retrieved from the state archives in Annapolis, where records more than ten years old are stored. The green manila folder arrived on my desk ten days later. I leafed through the case file. All of the records, reports, notes, and crime scene photos appeared intact. Millions of podcast listeners and true-crime fans would give anything to see what I held in my hands. Another story that may never be told. I locked Lee's case file in my desk for safekeeping, conveniently available in the event Syed is granted a new trial.

— CHAPTER FIVE —

THE NEXT ONE

In 2014, for only the second time since Richard Nixon's disgraced vice president, Spiro Agnew, was elevated to the statehouse nearly fifty years earlier, deeply blue Marylanders elected a Republican as governor. Larry Hogan was a fifty-eight-year-old real-estate developer from Annapolis. Son of a US representative with the same name, Hogan never before held an elected office. His only government experience was serving as appointments secretary — in charge of shepherding political appointees — for the previous Republican governor, Robert Ehrlich.

Hogan's upset victory in the 2014 election was part of a red-state wave that swept Republicans into governorships in Florida and Wisconsin and gains in state legislatures across the country. An anti-tax and anti-government sentiment animated conservative politics. As a candidate, Hogan promised to create a more favorable environment for business in Maryland.

"I'm all about trying to get government off our backs and out of our pockets," Hogan told diners at Mama's on the Half Shell, an oyster house in the hip east-side Baltimore neighborhood of Canton.

The day after being sworn in, Hogan unveiled a budget with wide-ranging cuts in funding for state agencies and programs, including reductions for education and aid for local governments.

State agencies, including the OCME, were subject to a 2 percent across-the-board cut in budget. I attended a meeting in which budget items — maintenance contracts, vacant staff positions, replacement of aging equipment, repairing lingering problems with the building — were weighed to make painful choices. Which were essential, which could be deferred, which could be thrown overboard to meet the budget target while maintaining buoyancy.

Hogan announced a freeze on the salaries of state employees, and a 2 percent raise we had received in January was going to be discontinued in July. He also began a voluntary separation program for state employees, offering a $15,000 payment and $200 for every year of service to those willing to leave their jobs. The state hoped to trim five hundred employees from its payroll, most of them older workers with considerable experience in their fields.

Like most people, before I worked at the OCME, I gave little thought to the medical examiner office. It's one of those things that exists in the background, like a sanitary sewer system or the electrical grid. It's always there, and we expect it to work correctly when we need it. The average person doesn't have a reason to think about it.

But when a public safety system fails, the consequences can be catastrophic.

Medical examiners don't just determine the cause and manner of death of individuals who die within a jurisdiction and sign death certificates for posterity, as important as that function is. The doctors also represent the dead, who can no longer speak for themselves, as fact witnesses in criminal proceedings.

In addition to playing this critical criminal justice role, the OCME is a bellwether of the public health system. Mortality data are used to measure the health of a population. It is important to know the cause and manner of death of all Marylanders and to have an accurate understanding of poisonings, domestic violence, impaired driving, and other issues. The medical examiner office is an early-warning monitor of trends in drug use and novel infectious diseases that might emerge in the community. Medical examiners in New Mexico were first to identify deaths from a previously unknown virus, hantavirus, in 1993. Based on an unusual cluster of four pediatric deaths in OCME data, former Baltimore City health commissioner Dr. Joshua Sharfstein spearheaded efforts that resulted in dangerous cold medication targeted for children being withdrawn from the market nationwide.

Throughout the United States, medical examiner offices tend to experience cycles of crisis. Some sort of scandal rocks an office. The chief medical examiner is fired or forced out. Public officials throw money at the problem and hire a new chief. Rinse and repeat. Scandals have plagued many medical examiner offices across the United States: New York City, Los Angeles, Boston, Chicago, Des Moines, El Paso, Fort Worth, the states of Connecticut, Delaware, Mississippi, and Virginia; the list goes on and on.

Many medical examiner and coroner offices reported a backlog of autopsies, sometimes holding bodies for days or weeks. At one point, the Los Angeles coroner office infamously had a backlog of three hundred to four hundred bodies awaiting autopsy. Families were unable to bury their loved ones according to religious custom or denied an open casket due to advanced decomposition. From Boston to Tulsa to the West Coast, families endured financial hardship during their period of grief because of delays in completing death certificates, sometimes for as long as a year. Without the final determinations, families are unable to access life insurance, bank accounts, burial benefits, Social Security survivor benefits. For too many families, the coroner or medical examiner made bad situations worse, compounding the distress of sudden and unexpected deaths.

The OCME is different. There has never been a backlog of autopsy cases. In almost every case, the decedent is examined within twenty-four hours of arrival at the OCME and ready for release to a funeral home the same day. If a person is Orthodox Jewish and must be buried before the next sundown, that's not a problem. The OCME runs like a finely tuned engine, with a record of stability and continuity stretching back decades. "It is the model medical examiner system in the United States," Fowler said.

People decry socialism, but they like socialized services in their everyday lives. We expect publicly funded police, fire, and emergency medical personnel to respond when we need them. We like our parks, libraries, and schools. We rely on air traffic control to keep us safe while traveling; we use global positioning and publicly regulated frequencies to post ironic memes to social media. Everything around us, from sewers to sidewalks and interstate highways, is publicly funded. Even the NFL with its billionaire owners is fundamentally a socialist enterprise, relying as it does on taxpayer support for stadiums, parking, transportation, and other essential infrastructure.

The public wants these things, but they don't want to pay for them with taxes. In the case of the OCME, the state's contribution is $12 million a year. Just as in Russell Fisher's day seventy years ago, it was still less than the state of Maryland spent on recreational fishing.

Companies across the country were telling employees to do more with less. Under Governor Hogan, the OCME's staff would have to do the same.

Katie Mingle, a producer for the *99% Invisible* podcast, visited in April 2015 to record an episode about the Frances Glessner Lee Homicide Investigation Seminar that is regularly held annually at the OCME. During the week, police officers practice crime scene observation skills with the collection of scale-model dioramas known as the Nutshell Studies of Unexplained Death.

My assignment was to accompany Mingle at all times while she was inside the building. I was to help her as much as possible within the confines of operational security while keeping her out of what would have constituted trouble for the OCME. Above all, I had to make sure that nothing was photographed or recorded that violated the privacy of a decedent or compromised the integrity of an investigation.

Mingle wore headphones and carried a digital audio recorder as we walked around the building. We took the stairs down to the third floor, where the laboratories are located. The OCME maintains its own in-house histology and toxicology labs. Histology involves slicing tissues into super-thin sections on a microtome, staining them to highlight various cellular structures, and putting them on a slide for the doctors to examine under a microscope. *Histology is the foundation of pathology*, Fowler told me.

We walked past histology to the bank of windows looking into the toxicology lab. Having in-house labs saves critical time in a forensic investigation. One-third of medical examiner offices in the country don't have toxicology labs. Samples have to be sent out to state or commercial laboratories, which can take weeks or longer to report results. The OCME's tox lab produces validated results in five days, a level of performance few medical examiner offices can match.

I opened the door to the neuropathology lab, where Troncoso, the neurodegenerative disorders expert, holds a weekly conference to examine brain and spinal cord specimens. Instruments are arranged on the stainless-steel counter lining the far wall. Windows to the left and right glowed with light from the two immense main autopsy rooms a floor below.

This balcony-level view is my preferred introduction to the autopsy area for civilians who don't have a lot of experience with dead bodies. It's self-limiting, allowing people to step toward the windows and let the view unfold as they feel comfortable.

Mingle walked toward the window without hesitation. She watched in silence.

On the day of Mingle's visit, OCME had thirteen bodies for examination. The circumstances or history of four of the dead, nearly a third of the day's caseload, suggested alcohol or drug use. Three were found in water; one was discovered floating in Chesapeake Bay, another in an Eastern Shore pond, and the third was a gentleman found decomposed in the bathtub, with the water running, of his Western Maryland home.

Two of the decedents were traffic fatalities, one an elderly woman who died in a single-vehicle crash and the other a man in his thirties who apparently suffered a seizure while driving. A man from the DC suburbs was found at home with an exposed wire hanging from the ceiling, which may or may not have been related to his death. Two of the decedents were killed by guns, including a young man from Baltimore City with multiple gunshot wounds and an apparent self-inflicted fatality from Southern Maryland.

Mingle observed the activity in the autopsy rooms. Groups huddled around gurneys with autopsies in various stages: bodies hollowed out and eviscerated, skulls truncated with the crown removed, exposing the intricate basilar structures. Doctors inspected organs, weighing and measuring, slicing specimens to retain in small plastic tubs of formalin.

"This is so weird," Mingle said. "It doesn't look anything like in the television shows. I never imagined so much would be going on, out in the open. I know this is real, but it looks fake. It looks like a movie set."

"Are you okay?" I asked.

"Yeah, I'm fine," she said.

"Want to go have lunch?"

"Sure," Mingle said.

"Let's go to Lexington Market."

We headed to the elevator to take it to the ground floor. The elevator door slid open to reveal Darrolyn Butler, an autopsy tech, leaning wearily against one corner. Butler is a big beefy guy with tattoos running down both arms. He wears a wireless headset over a do-rag, to listen to his postmortem playlist. Butler pushed the headphones off his ears and nodded as we entered.

"Hey, Darrolyn, how's it going?" I said, swiping my badge and pressing the button to go down.

"I'm standing upright and I have my clothes on," he said. "This is a good day."

"Rock on," I said, bumping his fist as he exited on the second floor.

During the week of Mingle's visit, disturbing video circulated on social media of a twenty-five-year-old man being arrested by Baltimore City police. The video showed Freddie Gray in handcuffs, limping toward a transport van then stepping up and through the rear door. The police van made four stops, once to remove Gray and place shackles on his ankles, then place him back inside facedown. By the time Gray arrived at the police station he had a severe spinal injury and was not breathing.

According to police, officers on patrol encountered Gray in Gilmor Homes, a public housing project in the Sandtown-Winchester neighborhood in West Baltimore. When Gray made eye contact with them, police said, he began to flee. Cops tackled Gray and arrested him for possession of a knife that turned out not to be illegal.

Some said the police gave Gray a "rough ride," also known as a nickel ride — driving erratically, stopping and accelerating rapidly, turning quickly, causing the handcuffed and unrestrained prisoner to tumble around the steel cage in the back of the vehicle.

This wasn't the first time people had been seriously injured while being transported by police. In 1997, Jeffrey Alston had been stopped by police for a speeding ticket and allegedly thrown headfirst into the transport van with his hands cuffed behind his back. Alston sustained a spinal injury, resulting in quadriplegia. The city settled his lawsuit for $6 million. Alston died in 2005 from complications of paralysis. In November 2005, police arrested forty-three-year-old Dondi Johnson Sr., for alleged public urination. Handcuffed and unrestrained in the police van, Johnson arrived at the police station with devastating spinal injuries. He died two weeks later. Johnson's family was awarded $7.4 million in a lawsuit against the Baltimore Police Department, later reduced to $219,000.

On Mingle's final day in Baltimore, protesters gathered at the Baltimore Police Department's Western District station. The next day, Sunday, April 19, Gray died.

My phone and email blew up. For the next several days, I was bombarded by CNN, Associated Press, Fox News, all the networks, local and national newspapers, wire services, public radio, international press, bloggers, alternative media, independent journalists, anybody with a camera or keyboard. Cameras were set up on the sidewalk in front of the OCME. People came up to the fourth-floor reception desk to ask questions and verify information. Everybody got the same answer: We don't discuss cases under investigation.

The only reporters I gave any time to were Serge Kovaleski and Richard Oppel of *The New York Times*. They had questions about the OCME and how forensic investigations were done in Maryland, reasonable questions that deserved answers. I agreed to tell them what I could on background, with the understanding that the Gray investigation was off-limits. Kovaleski and Oppel seemed genuinely interested in understanding the lay of the land, so we talked for a while in the deposition room, a conference room near the lobby with a lectern and a display case of forensic artifacts and specimens.

With tensions building in Baltimore, barricades were set up around the Western District station, city hall, and the state's attorney's office, fortified by a heavy police presence. The OCME, however, had no additional security. No barricades, no cops, not even a security guard.

Inside the building, it was business as usual. No case is more or less urgent than any other. After every death, people are always waiting for answers; next of kin, police, prosecutors, insurance companies, child protective services. But every case is treated the same. Freddie Gray was 15-03640, one of fifteen autopsies conducted at the OCME on April 20, 2015. The case was assigned to Dr. Allan.

Baseless rumors were circulating in the press and social media. Some suggested Gray may have injured himself, intentionally or not. I read that the medical examiner was being pressured to call the death an accident, which was not true.

Oppel of *The New York Times* called me. "I've been hearing a lot about a bolt on the inside of the van, that Freddie Gray may have hit his head on that," he said. "I don't want to waste my time if it's nonsense. Is that worth pursuing?"

Nobody is served by amplifying misinformation. I gave some thought about how to phrase my response. "As a journalist, I wouldn't consider that line of inquiry productive," I said.

"That's good to know," he said.

"Do you know of any information about the case that has leaked from this office?"

"No, not a thing."

"That's right. People here are disciplined. They know better than talking out of school," I said. "Where do you suppose those rumors are coming from? The only people who would even have that information are the medical examiner, the state's attorney's office, and the police. Who benefits from stories in the media suggesting Freddie Gray hurt himself? I don't see how the state's

CHAPTER FIVE — page 94

attorney gains anything by spreading rumors. You can come to your own conclusion."

On Saturday, April 25, a group of more than a thousand protesters gathered in the Gilmor Homes area where Freddie Gray had been arrested. They marched two miles through West Baltimore's most distressed neighborhoods to city hall. Then they proceeded down Martin Luther King Boulevard, passing within two blocks of the OCME.

Heading east on Lombard Street, the protesters paused at Shock Trauma, where Gray died, for a moment of silence. Then it was on to Camden Yards, where the Orioles were playing against the Red Sox. The crowd shut down an intersection at the Inner Harbor. Confrontations erupted into violence between protesters and baseball fans at bars across the street from the ballpark. Trash cans were thrown, windows broken. Several police cars had their windows smashed and roofs stomped. As the crowd drifted away, a 7-Eleven near the Civic Center was looted.

Fortunately, the OCME was largely unscathed by any of the protests. There was little disturbance at the building during the week of unrest, except that a police crime scene vehicle parked out front on Baltimore Street was broken into and $9,000 of cameras and forensic equipment stolen. The police called and asked to park inside the building in the ground-floor garage from that point on, but their request was denied. What does it say about the safety of your workplace when even the police are reluctant to park outside of it?

Things changed on Monday, April 27, after Freddie Gray's funeral. Word spread on social media of a rampaging "purge." High school students gathered around Mondawmin Mall, throwing bricks and rocks at police in riot gear, who responded with tear gas and pepper balls. Riots broke out in several locations, including the area around Pennsylvania and North Avenues.

Liquor stores, pharmacies, and other businesses were looted. More than 140 vehicles were torched, along with fifteen buildings, including a CVS store and a new senior residential facility still under construction.

As I watched on television, a chilling thought went through my mind. The OCME building, for all its forward-thinking design and state-of-the-art security, had one alarming vulnerability: the stairwells. The ground-floor stairwell doors are locked to prevent somebody from entering the building, but none of the other doors from the second floor up have locks, so staff can easily walk from one floor to another. If one of those beautiful blue reflective windows at the street level is smashed, an intruder can have unfettered access to the entire building. There's no telling how much damage could be done — records compromised or destroyed, equipment stolen, criminal prosecutions derailed.

I wasn't the only one who realized the OCME had a glaring security problem. The next morning, we had an emergency meeting to talk about the stairwells. Installing swipe card readers on all the stairwells would cost $30,000 — money that didn't exist in the budget — and would involve a months-long bidding process. Equipping the doors with regular keyed locks would cost $3,000 and could be done immediately. But staff would no longer be able to take the stairs from floor to floor. Only the handful of staff with a master key, including me, would be able to unlock a stairwell door. Not an ideal situation, but there was no other option that wouldn't result in dozens of keys floating around.

Katie Mingle emailed me from her home in the San Francisco Bay area. "Things seem to be getting pretty heated in Baltimore," she wrote. "Did you guys rule on cause of death? Just wondering about your perspective."

"You know I can't talk about the investigation," I replied. "The police have already said publicly that they expect to have it wrapped up this week. That's probably right."

One final step before Gray's case could be unpended was the neuropathology report. Even though the nature of the spinal injury was obvious, the group of forensic pathologists would still defer to the opinion of the neuropathologist Troncoso, who specialized in the brain and spinal cord.

Billy Murphy, a prominent attorney who played himself in *The Wire*, had been retained to represent the Gray family. Murphy has a reputation as an aggressive and outspoken legal advocate. His firm retained a neuropathologist to provide an expert opinion about Gray's spinal injury.

We hear about a "second" or "independent" autopsy being conducted on a high-profile case, but these are misnomers. There is no such thing as a second autopsy. Organs are removed during the forensic autopsy. Specimens, and often entire tissues and organs such as the brain or neck structures, are retained by the medical examiner and not available for an outsider to examine. Photos may be available, but they aren't as good as looking at the actual tissue. The organs are placed in a red plastic bag, all jumbled together, sewn into the body cavity, and sent along to the funeral home. An expert witness is unable to observe the organs in their original condition and the relationship between injuries. The process and quality of results are not the same as the forensic autopsy.

The only independent autopsy is the one provided by the state, which has no vested interest in the outcome. The expert retained by an attorney is working for one side of a likely lawsuit and can hardly be called independent. An autopsy report by a state medical examiner includes all of the known facts. The expert's report does not have to be complete.

If a subject matter expert is retained for a second opinion in a timely manner, they are welcome to attend the autopsy and spend the day at the OCME. There are already dozens of doctors, students, and technicians present during morning rounds, so having one more person present isn't an issue. Cases are done by consensus anyway. During morning rounds and the afternoon conference, everybody should be seeing the same thing and reaching the same conclusions. If there are differences of opinion, those are the times to discuss them.

"The more eyes, the better," Fowler explained to me. "If everybody missed something, we should know about it."

Murphy's expert was invited to attend the neuropathology conference on Thursday, April 30, when Gray's case was being presented. That day, a well-dressed young associate from Murphy's law firm also showed up in the OCME's waiting room expecting to join the examination with the doctors. Fowler told me that the neuropathologist was welcome to attend, but not the lawyer. An attorney is not a subject matter expert and had no business sitting in on the conference, he said.

"When our guest arrives, bring him to neuropath," Fowler said. "Under no circumstances let that lawyer get past you. He stays here. No matter what he says, he is not going to be in that room. We're not going to delay for any reason. Not one more day. The city is a powder keg."

While I was sitting in the waiting room with Murphy's associate, he turned to me and said, "Autopsies are public, did you know that? It's actually in the law. Families have the right to view an autopsy."

He was wrong, but there was no need to argue the point. I've read the Annotated Code and COMAR forward and backward. An autopsy *report* is public, but family or a member of the public observing an autopsy? No way. I just nodded and scrolled through my phone as we waited for the neuropathologist.

Murphy's neuropathology consultant arrived. I asked him to sign in and walked him toward the elevators. The young associate began to follow. "Wait here," I told him. "I'll be right back."

When I escorted the Gray family's expert to the autopsy room, a dozen or so medical examiners and students, along with Fowler, were gathered around Troncoso, the neuropathologist, at the workbench. I glanced at the spinal cord specimen on a stainless-steel platter, a slender strand of gray tissue about twelve inches long.

When I returned to the lobby, Murphy's associate was waiting for me. "Are you taking me now?" he asked.

"No, you're staying here," I said.

"You can't do this," he protested. "I have a right to be present. It says so in COMAR."

"Sorry, no."

He sputtered, quickly scrolling through his phone, increasingly agitated. "You don't realize what you're doing," the associate said to me. "You're going to be in big trouble."

People will say things to you, Fowler warned me when I started this job. *They'll threaten you. They'll say you'll be fired or criminally charged. Nothing is going to happen to you. We're represented by the biggest law firm in town — the attorney general's office. Ignore threats. It's just bluster.*

"Okay," I told the young lawyer. He eventually left in a huff. By then his protestations were moot.

Allan's examination revealed that Gray had an unstable fracture/dislocation of two vertebrae in his cervical neck and a near transection of the spinal cord. She described it as a "high-energy injury" of the type seen in shallow-water diving incidents, where the head is abruptly struck while in a hyperflexed and rotated position.

Restraints were available in the vehicle but not used. An accident is an event that is unforeseen. It isn't unforeseeable for a vulnerable person to be injured while handcuffed and unrestrained in a police van. Because police failed to follow safety procedures, Allan categorized Gray's death as a homicide. Despite what some media reported at the time, there was never a question that Gray's death was anything but a homicide.

Efficient as ever, Allan had most of the autopsy report already written. It was just a matter of adding some material, Troncoso's report, and signing off. The autopsy report was hand-delivered to the office of Marilyn Mosby, state's attorney for Baltimore City.

When I arrived at work on Friday, May 1, a dozen Maryland State Police officers stood several feet apart across the front of the OCME, their vehicles imposingly lined up along Baltimore Street. Finally, some security. When it no longer mattered. "Gee thanks, guys," I muttered as I walked past them to the entrance.

That morning, a story by Stephen Janis on the Real News website appeared on my Google News alert. "Freddie Gray Supporters Wary of Maryland Medical Examiner," the headline read. Although the headline was phrased as a plural, the article only quoted one source critical of the OCME, prominent civil rights attorney A. Dwight Pettit, who represented the family of Tyrone West. The single source was a plaintiff's lawyer in litigation with the City of Baltimore, hardly a disinterested observer. Janis's article had several major errors of fact and cited a "preliminary report from the Medical Examiner's Office" that didn't exist. The OCME doesn't report preliminary findings.

Most troublesome was a quote from Pettit. "When they do these autopsies, people are not aware, the police department's sitting right in the autopsy room," he said. "They have four, five, six, seven police officers sitting there right while the doctor's doing this. And so many cases you have that pervasive intimidation again, even in the Medical Examiner's office."

This is absolutely not true. Police are not in the autopsy room while work is going on. How are they going to intimidate a medical examiner? Janis didn't do the most rudimentary fact checking. I could have told him. Any homicide cop could have told him. It's a verifiable fact.

The article was baseless and recklessly inflammatory, throwing fuel on a very tense and volatile situation. Janis was giving people a reason to get angry, and pointing them at the OCME. He put a target on my back.

Mike Eagle and I gathered around Fowler's desk and watched a livestream of Mosby holding a press conference in War Memorial Plaza in front of city hall.

"The findings of our comprehensive, thorough, and independent investigation, coupled with the medical examiner's determination that Mr. Gray's death was a homicide, which we received today, has led us to believe we have probable cause to file criminal charges," she told the crowd. Her words were met with cheers.

I felt a tremendous sense of relief. "Glad that's behind us," I said to Fowler. "It's over."

"Until the next one," he said. "There's always a next one."

The next day, Allan came to my office and handed me a gift-wrapped six-pack of craft beer. Technically a violation of the ban on alcohol in state office buildings, I could plausibly deny knowledge of the contents of her gift until I opened it later at home. But the clinking gave it away.

"I wanted to thank you for everything you did during the last couple of weeks," she said. "You took all the heat from the media. I didn't have to deal with anything and was able to focus completely on the work."

I wasn't expecting that. I guess she thinks I'm okay after all.

I emailed Stephen Janis and invited him to meet me at the OCME. I intended to tour him through the facility and explain how forensic investigations work, as I had done with other reporters, giving him glimpses of morning rounds and afternoon conference. I wanted to discuss his issue with undetermined manner of death. A better understanding of the OCME might inform his work and result in more accurate and responsible reporting.

We made an appointment to meet at the OCME on May 5. He postponed our meeting, then postponed again. Ultimately, Janis never did meet with me.

Settling in to work on a pile of mail, I opened a fresh bag of Utz dark pretzels, my favorite, and set them aside on my desk as I munched and opened envelopes. One of the autopsy techs, Raymond Zimmerman, dropped by the chief's office for a visit. I had gotten to know and like Zimmerman, a West Baltimore native and one of the autopsy old-timers who'd seen everything.

"Utz pretzels, they're the best," he said, his hand diving into the open bag, rummaging around and withdrawing a fistful of salty deliciousness. Wearing a white lab coat over his blue scrubs, he leaned against my desk. He kept helping himself to more pretzels while we chatted, and then he left to return to the second floor.

Once the door closed behind Zimmerman, I looked at the bag of pretzels. I'm sure he's scrupulous about hand-washing, and anyway he wears gloves while doing autopsies. The lab coat looked clean, but he wore it in the autopsy suite. It had cadaver molecules on it. I couldn't get past the thought that hands that were inside a dead body plunged into my bag of pretzels. I threw the bag into the trash can.

A huge amount of postal mail is addressed to the chief medical examiner. Every document is date-stamped when it is received. Any mail that wasn't clearly for a specific department, and anything addressed to the chief or Fowler by name that wasn't obviously personal mail, was directed to me.

Stacks of subpoenas and requests for records crossed my desk and got shuttled to other people. Medical examiners are regularly called to testify in criminal trials — murders, vehicular homicides, criminal negligence and neglect. One of my duties includes tracking subpoenas on a Google Calendar. I was on top of every murder trial in the state. Needless to say, my box in the mailroom was often stuffed full.

I handled requests from family members and attorneys, complaints and questions about investigations, students working on class projects, letters from prisoners, novelists asking for realistic details for murder mysteries, and a staggering variety of odd correspondence. If somebody complained to their elected state lawmaker or the governor's office or the secretary of health about the OCME, that complaint got sent to me. Sometimes I had to check with Fowler for an answer, but in time I learned enough to resolve issues without bothering him.

My job involved serving sort of as the OCME's concierge, reliably trusted to handle matters that were out of the ordinary and to be a liaison for VIPs and other outsiders. Becoming friends with Susan Baker was an unanticipated perk of the job. I first met her soon after joining the OCME when she visited to have her photo taken with Fowler. Giddy as a fanboy, I told Baker how much her work has influenced my life. My well-worn copy of *The Injury Fact Book*, which she co-authored, still has a place on my home office bookshelf. I became Baker's contact person at the OCME. When she wanted to visit, I arranged for her parking in the first-floor garage and accompanied her upstairs. The octogenarian Baker remained an active researcher, periodically emailing me with requests for mortality data.

With so much time on their hands, inmates in prisons and correctional facilities were frequent correspondents. Most were tied to cases involving violent deaths; most were lifers. When I received a letter from a prisoner, I'd look up news stories about their crimes. Their letters often used language cribbed from law books at the prison library and the wisdom of jailhouse lawyers. Prisoners wrote to request records, photographs, and other documents such as policy and procedure manuals. Most of them were investigating their own cases. A few, I suspect, wanted photos to revel in their exploits. They wouldn't get photos, or any records aside from an autopsy report, without a court order or subpoena.

I read a meandering letter addressed to King, my office neighbor, from a resident of the Jessup Correctional Institution. He sought King's help to settle a jailhouse dispute about bullet wounds, basically whether shooting a person lying on the ground in the top of the skull would appear the same as or different from shooting a person who is standing but bent over at the waist. The prisoner directed his query to King because King was the medical examiner who testified at his trial. What better authority than the guy responsible for getting you locked up? Also, King was the only medical examiner he knew by name. For a kicker, he said that ten bucks at the prison commissary was riding on the answer. I respected the guy's creativity to settle a bet. But I told him the OCME's medical examiners don't comment on hypotheticals.

Several times a week I received long and convoluted emails from a man by the name of William Malone who claimed he was under FBI surveillance because he had information of national security interest. The emails were cc'd to dozens of addresses, including the US attorney general, senators, US Supreme Court justices, and numerous media personalities.

Malone claimed that former CIA director William E. Colby was assassinated on April 27, 1996, when he vanished while canoeing on the Wicomico River near his Southern Maryland home. The seventy-six-year-old Colby was found nine days later prone on a marshy shoreline. An autopsy determined that Colby suffered a heart attack, tumbled from his canoe, and died of drowning and hypothermia. The manner of death was ruled accident.

According to Malone, Colby was assassinated for airing the CIA's dirty laundry in the 1970s. He was killed in a way that looked like natural causes, he said. That's how you know the

agency did it. Furthermore, he continued, Smialek was assassinated the same way to cover up Colby's assassination. No wonder
Malone was concerned, with all that killing going on.

During lunch at the chief's conference table, I told Fowler
about Malone's wacky conspiracy theory emails.

"Colby? Nice older gentleman with a bad heart," Fowler said.
"That wasn't Smialek's case, that was mine."

"The CIA took out the wrong medical examiner?" I asked.

"Apparently so," he shrugged.

I scooted my chair to the far end of the table.

A man from the Eastern Shore wrote a letter with detailed
instructions for his cryopreservation upon his death. Two typed
pages gave step-by-step directions for preparing his body, infus-
ing an intravenous solution, and lowering his body temperature
with liquid nitrogen. It was absurd. The OCME can't do anything
like that. We don't even have IV infusion sets. It isn't as though
we could keep his instructions on file somewhere until he
showed up. Medical examiners don't take reservations.

I wrote him back and explained that by the time a person is
brought to the OCME they have been dead for hours or days —
far too late for resuscitation or cryopreservation. The procedure
he had in mind must be done immediately upon death. To do
that, I explained, he'd have to arrange to die in a hospital while
under a doctor's care, and good luck with that.

A woman wrote with concerns about the identification of her
husband, who had drowned while boating on the Patuxent River
in Southern Maryland in 1963. He was nineteen years old at the
time of his death. The couple had only been married a few months.
She was pregnant with their child. Life went on for her, if fitfully.

Discrepancies in the autopsy report bothered the widowed
bride. Now, decades later, little details fed vague doubts lingering
in her mind, always in the background, like an itch that couldn't
be scratched. The autopsy report recorded his height as six feet,

two inches, and his weight as 172 pounds. According to his driver's license, he was six feet four inches and weighed 185 pounds. His scalp hair was described as long in the autopsy report, with body hair "normal in distribution and amount." The woman said in her letter that her late husband had short hair on his head and "a body as hairy as an ape."

"It has taken me 50 years to try to find someone to provide me with some information," she wrote. Friends told her too much time had passed, better to leave it alone. But she had to know. Was the body that had been recovered from the river really her husband?

The mind isn't always reasonable. Grief often makes people cling to the most irrational of possibilities. If that wasn't your husband, where has he been hiding all this time? Did he fake his death with a look-alike body that hasn't been reported missing and is alive somewhere with an assumed identity, cutting off all ties to his past?

I had to be delicate in my response. A person's height when they are standing upright and cooperating may be different from that of a body measured in rigor mortis lying on a gurney. A difference of an inch or two is not surprising. Same thing with the weight. Things happen when a body is in the water, such as getting nibbled by fish and crabs. A couple of pounds' difference is no big deal. "Long" and "short" are subjective descriptions. The hair will look different when a body has been submerged compared with when a person is properly groomed. None of these things cast doubt on the dead man's identity.

Your husband was positively identified by the police, I wrote back to her. The police use a variety of means to identify a person, including fingerprinting and visual identification. I didn't know how he was identified, but it had certainly been done to the satisfaction of the medical examiner. That I knew for sure. If she had further questions about the identification of her late husband, they should be directed at the agency that made the ID — the Calvert County Sheriff's Office.

I said that I hoped she'd get a definitive answer and find peace someday. But I knew she probably wouldn't. Some wounds never heal.

Statistics for 2015 were grim. The OCME conducted 12,457 investigations during the year, a 25 percent increase from two years earlier. Medical examiners performed 4,626 autopsies — 500 more than the previous year. That was enough work for two more doctors in order to remain within NAME accreditation limits. Although one medical examiner was hired during the year, another took medical leave and died of cancer. Relative to the increased workload, the OCME was more thinly staffed than it had been a year earlier. Instead of asking to hire one medical examiner, Fowler should have asked for three.

Officially, using creative accounting, the OCME conducted an average of 312 autopsies per medical examiner, which is only a Phase I violation of NAME accreditation standards. In truth, three-quarters of the medical examiners were doing more than 325 autopsies per year, and more than half performed in excess of 400 autopsies.

Much of the growth in cases was due to gun violence and opioid drug deaths. Across the state, homicides jumped to 606 in 2015, up nearly 50 percent from the 414 deaths the previous year. Fueled by the spread of the lethal opioid fentanyl, there were 1,370 drug intoxication deaths — a 50 percent increase in two years.

Baltimore was particularly violent in 2015, whether due to pent-up rage, drug disputes, or, as many suspected, a work slow-down by police in the wake of Freddie Gray's death. The city experienced a record number of homicides, with the 344th and final homicide of 2015 occurring on New Year's Eve within feet of the front door of the OCME at West Baltimore and Poppleton.

CHAPTER SIX

AN ABUNDANCE
OF CAUTION

The wife of a foreign diplomat died of drug intoxication at her residence in the affluent Washington suburb of Chevy Chase, Maryland. Her family intended to fly her body back to their home country for burial. To ship a body internationally, the funeral director must have a non-contagion letter — a document certifying that a body is free of infectious disease and is safe to transport across international borders. Because it was Dr. Donna Vincenti's case, she had to sign the non-contagion letter.

Vincenti was downstairs in the autopsy suite, so I generated the non-contagion letter in CME and took the printed document on a clipboard for her to sign. Another medical examiner, Dr. Russell Alexander, rode the elevator along with me to the second floor.

"How is it going, Dr. Alexander?"

"Another day in paradise," he sighed.

"I know what you mean."

Blue paper booties over my shoes, I stood across the autopsy table from Vincenti and handed her the non-contagion letter with the pen beneath the clip. She removed her gloves and signed the letter, set my pen on the clipboard, and handed it back. The pen rolled off and fell into the hollowed-out cavity of the body between us. We looked at each other and peered down to my pen resting in a puddle of blood next to the vertebral column.

Damn. That was a Pilot G2 medium-point gel pen with blue
ink, my preferred writing implement. They're near impossible to
find with blue ink in retail stores. I really liked that pen.

"I guess I'm done with my pen now," I said.

"Sorry about that," Vincenti said, putting on a fresh pair of
gloves.

A disturbing number of people want to view or be around
dead bodies. I'm not one of them. Being around the dead doesn't
bother me, but it isn't something I seek out.

I often receive calls and emails from people asking to volunteer at the OCME or shadow a medical examiner. These requests
are routinely denied. Callers have asked whether they can come
watch an autopsy, as though the OCME were on the list of attrac-
tions like the Hershey's Chocolate factory tour.

Some visitors are fetishists who romanticize death, with gothic
accoutrements and morbid themes of coffins and graveyards
posted on social media. This fascination is a way, for some people,
of dealing with their own mortality. People who visit the Nutshell
Studies of Unexplained Death often tell me stories about murders
or the deaths of their family members, assuming that I have a
shared interest in all the gory details. I don't. This is just my job.

I received a call from a father of a daughter who wanted to
begin a course of study in forensic science at a community
college. Usually, this sort of call is about an internship, in which
case the answer would have been no. The OCME had stopped
allowing internships ever since, several years prior, an intern
took a picture of a body in the autopsy room and sent it to the
dead person's family. But this call was different.

"Before I spend money on her classes, I want to see if she has
the stomach for it," he told me. "I want to show her a dead body
and see if she throws up."

"That's the worst idea I ever heard," I said. "Not going to
happen here."

A couple of times a month I'm contacted by somebody interested in arranging a Scared-Straight-type encounter for wayward youth, inspired by the program from the late 1970s that attempted to turn at-risk kids into respectable members of society by frightening them with a taste of prison life. In some places, kids are brought into a morgue to look at dead bodies. Exposing a teen to the consequences of violence, the reasoning goes, may dissuade them from driving while intoxicated or pursuing a criminal lifestyle.

Although well intended, there is no evidence that these programs actually change behavior. The National Association of Medical Examiners has officially taken a position in opposition to using autopsy viewings as a form of punishment or deterrence. Perhaps most important, the dead who pass through the OCME never consented to have their bodies used for shock value.

"Decedents brought to this building didn't choose to be here," Fowler said to me. "People are here because they have to be. They haven't consented to anything. We have a duty to maintain their privacy and dignity."

"Come down to my office," Brian Tannenbaum, the OCME's network specialist and security guru, texted me. "You have to see something."

The OCME's new forensic medical center was literally built around IT. As soon as the concrete floors were poured, before the interior walls were framed, Fowler marked an outline in chalk on the fourth floor for the IT department. He and Mike Eagle moved in a desk and began designing and installing the IT system as the building was constructed around them.

"We practically lived there during construction," Eagle told me.

Fowler's interest in computerization dates to the early 1990s, when Smialek allowed Fowler to install the OCME's first network in the old Penn Street building and begin development of what would become the CME.

Eagle is in charge of a three-person department. In addition to Tannenbaum, William Spencer-Strong is a programmer who works on the CME and electronic infrastructure. Like Eagle, Spencer-Strong is also a Baltimore County firefighter.

The new building is totally independent from the state's technology infrastructure, with its own servers and email, so the OCME doesn't rely on the state's unreliable IT staff or suffer outages beyond its control. Fowler and Eagle incorporated some innovative features into the new building — RFID chips on case files so records can be located anywhere in the building, bar-code bracelets for bodies rather than toe tags, secure Wi-Fi networks, and dozens of security cameras covering critical areas of the facility.

I made my way to the IT department, cluttered with computers and peripherals, cables, phones, and assorted electronic gadgets. Behind a glass door, in a refrigerated room, stacks of servers hummed. Tannenbaum cued up security video on his monitor. He played a recording of four people walking through the OCME's front door and into the lobby. One was carrying a camera.

"We had a security breach," Tannenbaum said. "That's an HBO film crew. They went into the autopsy suite."

Oh shit.

Sonja Sohn, who portrayed Detective Shakima "Kima" Greggs in *The Wire*, was producing a documentary, *Baltimore Rising*, about Baltimoreans struggling to keep the city together in the wake of Freddie Gray's death.

On the afternoon of Saturday, January 30, 2016, a camera operator and producer working on Sohn's documentary accompanied two Baltimore City homicide detectives as they visited the OCME. The detectives signed in at the front desk, and a forensic investigator issued them visitor swipe cards. The investigator noticed the camera but assumed it was not being used since the cops know the rules. Signs prohibiting photos and video are posted in the lobby and on the doors leading to secure parts of the facility.

The group proceeded into the autopsy suite. The detectives went into the autopsy room to speak with a medical examiner. No autopsies were being performed at the time, but there are often bodies and body bags outside the autopsy rooms in the accession area leading to the body elevators. For a thirty-minute period, the HBO crew was out of view of the surveillance cameras, possibly in the gallery of the East autopsy room, where there are no security cameras.

Next, the group could be seen in the hallway outside the West autopsy room, running into Southall as she stepped off the elevator. She questioned them and ordered them out of the building. The HBO crew and the homicide detectives left through the ground-floor lobby, but it appeared the camera operator turned something on or off as they exited the building. Nobody knew what they might have recorded while they were inside.

Fowler directed me to get in touch with Sohn and make sure whatever video they recorded never saw the light of day. Legally, the OCME had little in the way of leverage to prevent the images from being broadcast. A provision in COMAR prohibits anybody from being in the autopsy area without the permission of the chief medical examiner or his designee, but it doesn't allow for any specific penalty. But filming a dead body without consent is an invasion of privacy that could put HBO, and the OCME, at risk of liability.

I was a big admirer of Sohn's work in Baltimore. Like Wendell Pierce, who played William "Bunk" Moreland, and others from *The Wire* cast, Sohn remained engaged with the city after the series ended. Sohn founded a non-profit, ReWired for Change, to help empower at-risk youth and families. The previous summer, my wife and I attended "Wired Up," an event Sohn organized at the Lyric Opera House, where cast members read monologues written by residents of Freddie Gray's Sandtown-Winchester neighborhood.

I'd hoped to someday interview Sohn for my website, Welcome to Baltimore, Hon. It was on my to-do list, but this breach and my assigned role in damage control meant that will never happen. From now on, I'll just be that asshole from the medical examiner office.

Through readily available information, I contacted Sohn's agent and expressed concern about the HBO crew's visit to the OCME. I received an email from Sakira Wang, Sohn's daughter, requesting an interview with Fowler. This was not going in the right direction.

"Dr. Fowler declines an interview," I replied.

Sohn followed up with an email assuring me that none of the footage shot at the office would be used. She apologized and repeated the request to interview Fowler.

I thanked Sohn for her consideration and said no to the interview.

The crew's access breach was a Baltimore police screwup, so we put it on them to make things right. Whatever agreements the police might have with a film crew do not extend to the OCME. The cops should have known better. Allowing the HBO crew in was a serious security violation. To make sure that the point got across clearly, I drafted a letter to go over Commissioner Davis's signature with all of the sternly worded bluster I could command.

Publication of the film or images may subject the film crew to criminal and civil penalties. Any video or audio material recorded at the OCME is not covered by permissions granted by the Commissioner of Police.

Should HBO release or broadcast any unauthorized material recorded at the OCME, they do so at their own peril.

No video from within the OCME was included when *Baltimore Rising* aired on HBO.

March 29, 2016

On the morning conference sheet, I read about Thomas Lemmon, a sixty-nine-year-old retired truck driver who was sitting in his prized Cadillac listening to music while his friend Daron Johnson sipped a beer in the passenger seat. They were parked on North Payson Street, a few blocks west of the OCME, just enjoying the day.

Without warning, the wall of 900 North Payson, one of Baltimore's thousands of crumbling vacant buildings, collapsed into the street and onto the car. Johnson managed to survive, but Lemmon was crushed to death by the bricks and debris.

Watching Fowler at work was fascinating. I don't mean as a medical examiner, but rather as chief of the office. He tended to stay at his desk, and medical examiners would visit to seek his advice throughout the day. No matter how unusual or confounding a situation, the chief could invariably refer to a policy or law that guided how to proceed. His command of forensic pathology was encyclopedic, and yet Fowler never argued with medical examiners over their cause and manner of death determinations. "I give them their professional freedom," he said.

He reviewed all homicides, deaths of children and infants, and cases of undetermined manner of death, but only to make sure the medical examiners had been thorough and complete. If the facts supported a medical examiner's conclusion, the cause and manner of death determinations were left to their judgment. "The conclusion of an autopsy report is labeled 'opinion' for a reason," he said to me. "That's their opinion, and I'll back them up."

Fowler was respected for his performance as a fact witness in court. His testimony was concise, strictly within the confines of what he knew for certain. "Defense lawyers do their very best to make you look stupid or incompetent," he said, but he was unflappable. He had been cross-examined by some of the best.

One Monday morning I arrived at work with the fingernails on my left hand painted with black glitter polish. Over the weekend we had visited with my wife's brother and his family, where my young daughter and even younger niece delighted in painting my nails. My manicure looked like the work of somebody with a neurological disorder. When we returned home, I tried to remove the nail polish with acetone only to find that the glitter would not come off. The kids were supposed to apply a clear layer beneath the glitter. Bits of plastic impervious to acetone were now glued to my nails. So I gave up trying to remove the nail polish and went to work the next day with glittery painted nails.

Eating lunch at Smialek's rustic wood table, Fowler took notice. "Had your nails done?" he asked.

"It was done to me."

"Oh?" he said, setting down his fork. "You were walking down the street minding your own business when a group of strangers randomly assaulted you, held you down, and painted your nails?"

"No sir," I admitted. "It didn't exactly happen that way."

"Then you had them done," he said, satisfied by making his point and returning to his meal.

Every day was like a seminar. Fowler, Rodriguez, and Brown,

the administrator, often had lunch around Smialek's table. The conversations ranged from ballistics to shaken baby syndrome and decompression injuries during scuba diving. Proximity to specialized knowledge gave me an opportunity to get answers to the kinds of questions people are always asking, such as what is the deal with feet washing up on shore in the Pacific Northwest? People on the internet claim there is a perverse serial killer on the loose.

"It's really quite simple," Fowler said. "When somebody drowns or jumps off a bridge, critters in the water do their work and eat up the soft parts. The last bit remaining is the foot, which is held together by several ligaments and protected by a shoe. Often it is an athletic-type shoe, which is buoyant, so it floats to the surface and washes ashore."

Sure. It makes perfect sense. Once it's explained.

For a while Fowler was eating a sort of paleo diet, types of food similar to what sustained early humans. He swore off the hot dog cart parked by the front door and brought in containers of minimally processed vegetables and whole grains.

"You know they had a life expectancy of thirty years back then," I remarked.

"But it was a hell of a ride," he replied. "Actually, the data are skewed by deaths during infancy and childhood. If you survived to adulthood, life expectancy wasn't terribly different from what it is today. Many people lived to a ripe old age."

I knew that. I asked him if he had given any thought to retiring. Fowler had been chief since 2001 and by then, 2016, was fully vested in the state pension system. Although the state has no mandatory retirement age, Fowler would hit the sixty-five milestone within a few years.

"I wouldn't wait too long if you want to have any retirement life, to have the time to travel and do the things you want to do,"

I said. "Maldeis died of cancer while in office. Fisher lived for about three weeks after retirement. And then Smialek. The long-term prospects for chief medical examiners don't look all that good. I'm just saying."

Working at the OCME allows me to sit in on training programs — a bloodstain analysis workshop taught by members of the Baltimore City homicide squad, forensic anthropology by experts from the Smithsonian's National Museum of Natural History.

The annual homicide investigation seminar is especially worthwhile, with sessions on various trauma deaths resulting from bullets, blades, and blunt objects. Most of the attendees are homicide detectives, with a smattering of prosecutors, FBI agents, NCIS, and other investigators from agencies throughout the United States and around the world.

One of the highlights of the homicide seminar is a presentation by an FBI behavioral analyst, a real and important job that gets highly fictionalized as a profiler in books and movies like *The Silence of the Lambs*. In other sessions, Fowler walks the seminar attendees through the process of a forensic autopsy, and Ripple, a deputy chief, presents a session on excited delirium and in-custody deaths, one of her areas of interest.

For that year's seminar, Ripple showed cell phone video of a recent incident in Prince George's County, a case still under investigation. The video begins with a thirty-two-year-old Black man standing, shirtless, in the bed of a pickup truck in the parking lot of an apartment complex. A few neighbors have gathered nearby to observe the activity and can be heard off-camera. The man holds a large rock over his head and gestures as though threatening to throw it. Two police officers stay at a distance, trying to speak with him, but the man is unintelligible. He is in the throes of a toxic brew of mental illness and drugs — cocaine, phencyclidine, methamphetamine, who knows what — and is agitated beyond reasoning. Pacing aimlessly, constantly moving, he grunts and barks.

Whooping and laughter can be heard coming from off-camera. The person shooting the video, as well as other residents of the apartment complex, are goading the man on.

"Go on, dawg," a voice said on the video.

"Go on, dawg," somebody echoed in the darkened conference room. The cops chuckled like middle-school students.

Ripple was not amused. "You can laugh," she said. "You're watching the last minutes of a man's life."

The room fell quiet as we watched the man repeatedly jump in and out of the truck bed. Officers tased him several times, to no effect. The man picked up a flowerpot and tried to throw it through an apartment window, but it bounced off the glass and fell to the ground. As he bent to pick it up, cops pounced and wrestled him down and had him handcuffed within seconds. By then, he was unresponsive. One moment he had been grunting and moaning, and then he wasn't.

Excited delirium is what medical people call a controversial diagnosis. Some doctors contend that it doesn't exist. They suggest that excited delirium is a convenient label fabricated to explain deaths in police custody that are really due to asphyxiation or choke holds.

My understanding from Fowler and other forensic pathologists is that excited delirium is real. A deadly combination of mental illness, psychoactive drugs, and an open floodgate of adrenaline leads to an uncontrolled cascade of neurotransmitters and a distinct cluster of signs and symptoms — most notably an extraordinarily high body temperature.

"If you look at the excited delirium literature, the body temperature is recorded as high as 108 degrees Fahrenheit," Fowler told me. "Do you know why it's always reported as 108 degrees?"

"No idea," I said.

"That's as high as clinical thermometers go," Fowler said. "Nobody really knows how high the body temperature reaches in excited delirium."

My wife, a registered nurse, used to work in labor and delivery at Baltimore's St. Agnes Hospital. When I spoke to groups touring the OCME, I liked pointing out that my family covers both ends of the life continuum, providing cradle-to-grave care. That was a reliable laugh line. Then my wife took a job at an outpatient urology clinic. I was happy for her, but the job forced me to come up with new urology-related material. I texted her:

> I'm having difficulty urinating.

Within minutes, she texted back.

> OMG, what's wrong? Weak stream? Incomplete emptying?

> I put my underwear on backwards this morning, The vent is in back. Very difficult to pee like that.

> LOL. Fix your underpants. You almost gave me a heart attack

My desk phone rang. It was Linda Thomas calling from the fourth-floor reception desk. "You have a gentleman here to read an autopsy report," she told me.

The OCME is required by COMAR to charge for certified copies of autopsy reports, $25 for first-degree relatives and $100 for all others. But because autopsy reports are public records, members of the public have the right to "inspect" them at a reasonable time and place. For some people, even $25 is too much of an expense. We let people read reports in person, but not keep them or make copies, at no cost.

My duties include accompanying visitors while they read autopsy reports, to make sure they don't make copies with a phone. I answer questions as I can, within limits. I may define terms — atherosclerotic cardiovascular disease means a heart attack or stroke, ecchymosis is bruising — but strictly avoid any interpretation or elaboration because I'm not qualified.

Sitting in a room with a person reading the details of their loved one's death is a peculiar experience. They often tell me stories about the dead person's life or the circumstances of their death, what they recall of that day. I listen patiently to these deeply personal accounts without judgment. Visitors want to find out about drugs found in the bloodstream, to confirm their suspicions. Often it is obvious that the person across the table had a drug relationship with the deceased, a roommate or boyfriend in a cluttered residence where foil wrappers, needles, capsules, and other paraphernalia were present. More than once, I was certain that my visitor was the person who supplied the drugs, and watched them process the realization that they are responsible for a death.

A middle-aged man wearing a sports coat and a familiar yellow necktie — I had one just like it — was waiting for me in the fourth-floor lobby. He was an attorney visiting the OCME for a personal matter. A couple of years before, his son, in his early twenties, shot a young woman in broad daylight in the parking lot of a strip mall. Then he shot himself in the head. They had been dating but had broken up. She'd agreed to meet him in a public place, a Starbucks. He was waiting for her in the parking lot, got into her car, and opened fire.

The father was remarkably composed while reading his son's autopsy report, showing no outward emotion. He explained that he had come to terms with his son's heinous act, but his family, his wife and daughter, still had some doubts about certain facts. They knew from the death certificate that he died from a gunshot wound but didn't know where on his body he'd been shot. The windows of the vehicle were open. Was there any possibility that the shots that killed them came from outside the vehicle? Was there any possibility, however slim, that their son and the young woman were both killed by random stray bullets?

The father read the report. His son's gunshot wound was under his chin and through the top of his head.

"Well, that's that," he said with finality.

When speaking with people experiencing the aftermath of trauma, it's important to consider their state of mind. For me, it's just another workday. But for a family member on the other end of the phone, it is one of the worst days of their life. They are in the midst of a life-altering event, experiencing the stress and range of raw emotions unexpected death leaves in its wake.

Information can take awhile to process. As you are speaking to a family member, they are trying to absorb unfamiliar terms and concepts. Thoughts are spinning in their head, raising more questions to ask. Not every word you say gets through.

I remind myself to speak slowly. Choose language carefully. Use as few words as possible. Keep it clear and direct, without elaboration. Only answer the question being asked, never volunteering information beyond that. It may be necessary to repeat things several times. If there is a pause in the conversation, whether to gather thoughts or stifle a sob, give it time. I'm ever aware that the visit or phone call is about them, not me.

Denial can be a powerful force to reckon with. One day a woman visited the office to read the autopsy report about her husband, who'd died two months earlier due to oxycodone intoxication. She came across as a professional, perhaps a lawyer or high school principal, somebody who had her act together. She was in her thirties, with a nice suburban home and two young children who had just lost their father. And she had no idea, two months after her husband's death, that opioids had killed him. She didn't even know that he used opioids.

"He died of a heart attack?" she asked, setting the report down on the table.

"No, he died from oxycodone intoxication."

"A heart attack?"

"No," I said, flipping the report open to the conclusion and pointing my finger to the line that read CAUSE OF DEATH: OXYCODONE INTOXICATION. "The cause of death was oxycodone intoxication."

"That causes a heart attack?"

"No, he did not have a heart attack. He died from a drug intoxication."

"What does that do? It doesn't cause a heart attack?"

"No," I replied. I shouldn't say anything beyond the cause and manner of death. I shouldn't explain or drift into an area of expertise. But it didn't seem right to tell her to Google it. "Opioid intoxication depresses the central nervous system. It makes a person get drowsy and stop breathing," I said.

She told me that she and her husband were high school sweethearts. "We knew each other since we were teenagers," she told me. "He's the only man I've ever been with. I've known him my whole adult life. We made a family together. We spent every day and every night together. I thought I knew him like I know myself."

The woman told me that her husband never drank, didn't smoke tobacco or marijuana, and was never known to use illicit drugs. He was even reluctant to take prescription medication.

"I had absolutely no idea he was using drugs," she said. "I just can't conceive of it. How is it possible? We lived together in the same house. Can a person have a whole other hidden side that you know nothing about?"

I thought about the secrets I hold in confidence. Some things I wished I didn't know. "Yes, people can have a hidden side," I told her.

Another time I sat with a woman as she read the autopsy report for her eighteen-year-old son, who'd died along with his best friend in a car crash. They were headed to her home when the car was T-boned by a truck that ran a red light. The woman's son was in the front passenger seat, directly where the truck struck the car. Neither of the kids had alcohol or drugs in their system. The truck driver faced criminal charges, but that didn't alter the fact that two young men were dead.

"They almost made it home," she told me. "The crash happened about half a mile from our house. We had just talked on the phone. The last thing he said to me was 'See you soon. Love ya.' At least I have that. 'See you soon. Love ya.'"

She read the autopsy report quietly, using a tissue to dab her tears. When she finished, she sighed deeply. "I need to know. Did he suffer? I can't bear the thought of my baby boy in pain."

Suffering is a loaded question. Pain and suffering are subjective matters squabbled over by expert witnesses in civil litigation. Suffering can't be quantified. But I understand. If it were my child, I'd ask the same question. I would wonder about their last moments, too.

I'm not supposed to do this. I'm not qualified to give an opinion.

I picked up the autopsy report and scanned the inventory of injuries the woman's son sustained. Fractures of the right arm and shoulder, both legs, and pelvis. Punctured lung. Lacerated liver and spleen. All devastating trauma. But two injuries stood out. He had a fracture dislocation of the first and second cervical vertebrae with transection of the spinal cord — a so-called internal decapitation — and the force of the crash ripped his aorta from its anchor on the chest wall, severing the body's main artery. Either one of these injuries will cause nearly instantaneous unconsciousness and death. Given the jolt of the crash and the spinal cord injury, he was stunned and dead faster than pain impulses can travel up the nerves.

I thought before speaking. "Honestly, I can't imagine a more painless death," I said to her. "He didn't feel a thing."

Gallery featuring framed photos of every medical examiner who has served at the OCME since its founding in 1939.

Canine members of Chesapeake Search Dogs serve as therapy animals while spending time visiting with OCME staff.

Baltimore's first purpose-built morgue, completed in 1890, was located on the waterfront adjacent to a flood-prone stream that served as an open sewer.

A modern morgue was built next to the city's sewage pumping station in 1925. This building at 700 Fleet Street served as the Baltimore Morgue, and later the Office of the Chief Medical Examiner, until 1969.

A second story was added to the Fleet Street building in 1947.

The Office of the Chief Medical Examiner building at 111 S. Penn Street, near the University of Maryland Medical Center campus, opened in 1969.

The OCME's 120,000-square-foot forensic medical center opened in Baltimore's BioPark in October of 2010. Occupying a city block, it is the largest freestanding forensic medical center in the US.

Dr. Russell Fisher, who served as chief medical examiner for the State of Maryland from 1949 to 1984, transformed the OCME into a leading center of training and research.

Dr. John E. Smialek, chief medical examiner from 1984 until 2001, at a press conference revealing the cause of basketball player Len Bias' death from cocaine intoxication, June 24, 1986.
Photo: Bill Smith/AP/Shutterstock

Dr. David R. Fowler, who served as chief medical examiner from 2001 until 2019, testified for the defense in the trial of Derek Chauvin, the former Minneapolis police officer convicted for the murder of George Floyd, April 14, 2021.

One of two main autopsy rooms. A grid of bright fixtures on the ceiling floods the rooms with so much light that no shadows are cast on the work areas, even when leaning over a table.

The main autopsy rooms have elevated galleries where homicide detectives and crime scene technicians wait for bullets, clothing, and other evidence. Only OCME personnel are in the autopsy room during examinations.

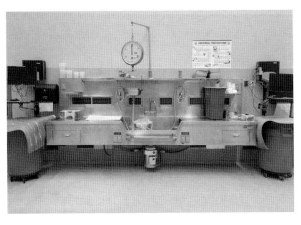

One of eight autopsy stations in each of the main autopsy rooms. With the six stations in the biosafety suite, the OCME can easily conduct 22 or more autopsies at once.

The OCME has three biosafety autopsy rooms under negative pressure to prevent a deadly infectious disease from escaping the facility. Each biosafety room has two stations, for a total capacity of six simultaneous autopsies.

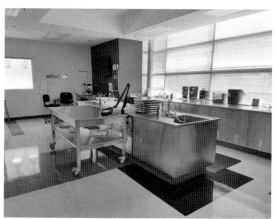

The OCME's neuropathology room, where brain and spinal cord are examined. Windows to the left and right look down into the main autopsy rooms one floor below.

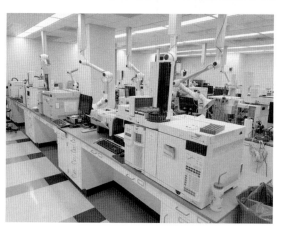

The OCME's in-house toxicology laboratory produces results quickly, in as little as five days. Deaths related to the powerful opioid fentanyl have contributed to a tripling of the lab's work in recent years.

The OCME's ground floor garage and receiving area has high-speed roll-up entrance and exit doors. The columns are equipped with water, drainage, electric, and internet access so the 20,000-square-foot area can be used for postmortem examination in the event of a mass fatality incident. Hundreds of bodies can be stored within the building.

A motorcade accompanying Prince George's County police officer Mujahid Ramzziddin leaving the OCME. Ramzziddin was shot off-duty while assisting a neighbor during a domestic dispute on February 21, 2018.

Baltimore activist, artist, and barbecue cook Duane "Shorty" Davis at a West Wednesday event, organized to protest the death of Tyrone West and other Black men while in police custody.

Tyrone West's sister, Tawanda Jones (second from right), at a West Wednesday protest at the OCME, February 26, 2014.

The author at a West Wednesday protest at the OCME, September 10, 2014, speaking with members of Tyrone West's family.

She rested her hand on mine. "Thank you," she said. "You have no idea what that means for my peace of mind. I hope I can sleep tonight."

I swallowed hard, struggling to keep my emotions in check. I don't know for certain whether her son suffered, but it was what she needed to hear from me. "I hope you get some rest," I said.

Heading back to my office, I encountered Donnell McCullough, the autopsy services supervisor. "You doing all right?" he asked.

"Man, I don't know if I'm feeling it today," I said.

McCullough put his arm around my shoulder and pulled in close. "I'm doing a delivery of tissue specimens to the crematory this afternoon," he said. "Go downstairs and pick yourself out a body bag. Zip yourself up, and I'll take good care of you."

"I know you would, Donnell," I said. "Thanks."

In the predawn darkness of November 1, 2016, school bus number 1876 was eastbound on Frederick Avenue through Irvington, a neighborhood about four miles west of downtown Baltimore. Operated by AAAfordable Transportation under contract to Baltimore City Public Schools, the bus was beginning its morning pickup route to bring special needs children to Dallas F. Nicholas Sr. Elementary School.

Teacher aide Robin Simon sat in the rear-facing seat directly behind the bus driver, sixty-seven-year-old Glenn Chappell. Simon kept attendance on a sheet of paper on her lap. So far, the morning was routine and on time. The student they were supposed to pick up at the first stop at 6:29 A.M. wasn't there. Bus drivers are instructed to wait three minutes at the bus stop then move on. Headed to the second stop of the morning, Simon was intently focused on the paperwork on her lap. She barely noticed the bus gaining speed and jostling down the street until she felt a sudden jolt.

Simon reflexively planted her foot to brace herself, grasped the seat in front of her, and began to turn around and speak to the driver when a deafening crash threw her back into the seat. The front end of the bus crushed, Simon struggled to her feet in the smoke-filled interior and worked her way to the rear exit. Glancing back at Chappell and seeing his injuries, she had no doubt he was dead. Not until she stepped outside the bus did the enormity of what happened become apparent.

The bus had caromed down Frederick Avenue, reaching fifty-seven miles per hour when it struck the rear of a white 2012 Ford Mustang being driven by a retired DC police officer, the impact pushing the sports car into the wall of Loudon Park Cemetery.

The bus kept going, barreling down Frederick Avenue for another nine hundred feet. As the road curved to the right, the school bus crossed the center line and struck a westbound Maryland Transit Authority bus with thirteen passengers aboard, scraping along the left side of the vehicle.

The transit bus driver, thirty-three-year-old Ebonee Baker, and four passengers were killed. Three passengers were seriously injured and transported to Shock Trauma.

One of the forensic investigators responding to the scene was Gray Maggard. Forensic investigators are the OCME's first responders, the eyes and ears for the medical examiner in the field. Like Maggard, most of the investigators are EMTs. Many have degrees in forensic science or criminal justice. Maggard is a former Department of Natural Resources police officer — the "fish fuzz," he jokes. His assignment was the Francis Scott Key Bridge across the outer harbor, a popular destination for those intent on suicide. Several times a year Maggard recovered bodies of those who jumped from the span, 185 feet above the water, and on rare occasions rescued the few who survived the lethal drop.

Today Maggard's task was helping to extricate victims from where physics sealed their fate. Damage to the vehicles showed the tremendous force of the impact. "One side of the MTA bus was ripped open, from front to back," Maggard told me later. "The side of the bus was peeled back like an aluminum can."

It seemed that everybody I knew had some connection to the Frederick Avenue bus incident. The crash happened near my home, on the route I use if I take the MTA to work. Baker, the MTA bus driver, was a high school track coach. Detective Edward Wilson, the OCME's liaison officer with Baltimore City Police Department, knew her from track meets. One of her passengers was a Department of Health employee. A forensic investigator knew another of the passengers.

The six fatalities were neighbors and friends. It could have been any one of us.

Within hours, reporters began digging into Chappell's background and driving record. The school bus driver had a history of diabetes and seizures. In the previous five years, he had been involved in at least a dozen crashes involving a school bus or personal vehicle. Some of these crashes involved seizure-like activity. EMS had even once responded to the AAAfordable company's offices when Chappell was having what witnesses called a seizure.

The autopsy revealed that Chappell died from multiple injuries in the crash. The manner of death was ruled accidental. Did he have a seizure while driving? There's no way to know.

The media pounced. Several news outlets called for clarification. I was determined to stay very narrowly on cause and manner of death, and say as little quotable as possible.

"It's being reported that the school bus driver died from multiple injuries," said a reporter from one of the local television stations.

"That's correct," I said.

"What caused the crash?"

"I don't know."

"It's also being reported that he had diabetes and seizures," the reporter said.

"Okay," I said. Tread carefully and avoid confirming information. Anything outside of the autopsy report is a confidential medical record. His medical history might have been irrelevant, for all I knew. Because the autopsy report hadn't been typed up yet, I didn't know what would be in it.

"Do you have any response to that?" he asked.

Why would I respond to that? "We don't discuss confidential medical information," I said.

"Was he unconscious when the bus crashed? Did he have a medical emergency?"

"I don't know," I said. "All I can tell you is that the cause of death is multiple injuries and the manner of death is accident."

And you're not going to get one word more than that out of me.

The first meal I ate in Baltimore when I moved here from Memphis was at the Double T Diner, a Catonsville landmark at the intersection of two of the area's busiest streets. My family has eaten there many times since. It's the sort of neighborhood place that everybody who lives in the area has been to at one time or another. The Double T has a steady business. On Sundays the restaurant is jammed.

In mid-December, between the holidays, a married couple sat in their pickup truck parked directly in front of the entrance of the Double T, pausing to snort what they thought was heroin before continuing with their day. But their heroin had been spiked with fentanyl. When the man lapsed into unconsciousness, his wife called 911. Paramedics rushed to the Double T and administered Narcan, a drug that reverses the effects of opiates. The man was taken by ambulance to St. Agnes for further treatment. Once sobered up, he was released and took a taxi back to his truck at the Double T. When he arrived, he found his wife's lifeless body in the passenger seat. Despite watching her husband overdose and nearly die, she'd snorted some of the same drug after he'd been taken away.

Until I worked at the OCME, I never knew of the remarkable diversity of substances with which people kill themselves. Nitrous oxide, also known as laughing gas and readily available in small metal canisters called whippets. Compressed air, the type used to clean keyboards. Bath salts and other exotic drugs. I'd never previously heard of anybody killing themselves by eating berries from a yew plant. I didn't even know that yew berries were poisonous. Then two cases came through the OCME just days apart.

By far, the most lethal drugs are the opiates — heroin, fentanyl and its analogs, prescription narcotics — often in combination with alcohol or cocaine.

I never before appreciated how often people die of alcohol and drug intoxication on special occasions, like birthdays, wedding parties, and spring break. Somebody is celebrating and having a good time, already has alcohol and who knows what else in their system, and a friend offers a tablet or line of powder to kick it up a notch. People die celebrating their release from rehab or jail. A month or two clean resets the body's drug tolerances. When veteran users take a hit of their customary dose, it's too much for their recalibrated system and they die. Aging baby boomers in their sixties and seventies sometimes cruised through narcotic addiction for years until running across a fatal fentanyl hotshot.

Drugs are overtaking lives across the spectrum of demographics — young and old, wealthy and poor, white and Black, urban to rural — throughout the state of Maryland.

The economics of opiates favor powerful drugs like fentanyl. Importing heroin through traditional smuggling methods costs about $25,000 per kilo. Factories located overseas are churning out fentanyl and other synthetic opioids by the ton. A kilo of pure fentanyl, fifty times more potent than heroin, can be ordered online and delivered undetectably in two days by express shipping for $2,500 or less. A small amount of fentanyl in a batch of mediocre heroin — or any sort of powder such as baking soda — becomes a marketable product in the streets. Fentanyl can also be pressed into bogus pills that look like legitimate prescription drugs.

Drugs and drug-related violence pushed the OCME's caseload further upward in 2016 — in excess of 14,300 investigations. That's four thousand more investigations than when I came on the job in 2012, nearly a 40 percent increase in four years. Narcotics were a major driver of the caseload, with more than twelve hundred of those cases due to opioid-related deaths during the year.

The OCME's medical examiners performed more than 5,300 autopsies during 2016, an increase of more than 1,200 in two years — enough work for four more doctors. They performed an average of 342 autopsies each, far above the level recommended by the National Association of Medical Examiners. All of the fifteen medical examiners exceeded the maximum limit of 325 cases per year, and ten of the forensic pathologists conducted more than 400 autopsies, a brutal workload.

The forensic pathologist hired last year, when we needed three additional medical examiners, went on extended leave in Europe and eventually resigned her position. Another medical examiner was hired, leaving the OCME still lacking in forensic pathologists.

There is a severe shortage of forensic pathologists available for hire across the country. An estimated four to five hundred forensic pathologists are in practice in the United States. Fellowship programs produce forty or fewer new forensic pathologists annually — not enough to replace those who retire or leave the profession, much less begin to fill the estimated present-day need of eleven hundred to twelve hundred qualified medical examiners. The forensic pathologist shortage is so severe that the National Association of Medical Examiners job bank has forty positions open, including a listing for the OCME of Maryland, which has been active since 2011.

The increase in OCME cases doesn't just translate into a need for more doctors; there is also a need for more autopsy technicians to work alongside them. More forensic investigators, more secretaries to produce more reports, and more clerks to handle more requests for records are also desperately needed.

But while cases at the OCME were climbing, staffing declined. The state's freeze on hiring meant that positions that became open through retirement were reclassified and transferred to other departments, from secretaries and support staff to investigations and the toxicology lab techs.

"When I started, every pathologist had their own secretary," Fowler told me. "Then it was one secretary for two doctors, and one secretary for three doctors. Look at us now. We have three secretaries handling all of the work for fifteen doctors."

According to surveys of other forensic medical centers, based on its volume of work the OCME of Maryland should have a staff of thirteen secretaries. With only three secretaries, reports are unavoidably delayed. Accreditation requires the OCME to complete 90 percent of autopsy reports within sixty days. The OCME fell far short of that goal in 2016 with only 64 percent of reports finished on time.

At the annual meeting of the Postmortem Examiners Commission, the OCME's governing body, Fowler told the board that the agency was in crisis and risked losing NAME accreditation. Work in the toxicology laboratory increased 300 percent in four years and was running tests twenty-four hours a day to keep up.

The OCME desperately needed more, Fowler told members of the commission: more forensic investigators, more autopsy technicians, more laboratory personnel, and, most of all, more forensic pathologists. Things were getting worse and reaching a breaking point. The status quo was unsustainable.

It was pretty much the same report he had given to the Post-mortem Examiners Commission the year before and the year before that. Things had just kept getting worse.

As the drug deaths spiraled upward, a new synthetic opioid appeared on the streets in the autumn of 2016 — carfentanil. A hundred times more potent than fentanyl, a dose of carfentanil as small as a single grain of salt can be fatal.

— CHAPTER SEVEN —

COPS AND ROBBERS

The Baltimore Police Department, still bruised by the aftermath of Freddie Gray's death in 2015 and a subsequent US Department of Justice investigation into civil rights abuses, was rocked by another scandal in March 2017 when seven police officers were indicted on federal charges of racketeering, conspiracy, and a slew of other crimes.

The seven cops were members of an elite squad tasked with seizing illegal guns, known as the Gun Trace Task Force. On the streets of Baltimore, the GTTF was a roving gang of bandits with guns and badges — "1930s-style gangsters," as Police Commissioner Kevin Davis described them. Members of the GTTF robbed and extorted people, stole drugs and resold them, planted weapons, and inflicted abuse on communities of color.

One of the tactics used by the GTTF was "door pops" — suddenly pulling up to a group of people congregating on a sidewalk and throwing open the vehicle's doors. If anybody ran, the task force members gave chase. This type of maneuver ensnared Freddie Gray.

A month after the GTTF officers' arrest, the city entered into a consent decree with the US Department of Justice. The subsequent federal investigation revealed that the police department

had engaged in a pattern of practice and conduct that violated
the civil rights of citizens.

According to the Department of Justice, the Baltimore police's
zero-tolerance enforcement strategy resulted in illegal stops,
searches, and arrests. The police used unreasonable force and
overly aggressive tactics, disproportionately targeted the African
American community, and retaliated against people exercising
their right to free expression.

In other words, the police were doing the things critics had
been accusing them of doing for years.

Maryland is the only state that gives family members the right to
appeal a medical examiner's cause and manner of death determinations. COMAR and state law include provisions allowing a
"person in interest" — defined as a parent, child, sibling, or
guardian — to request that the medical examiner change the
cause or manner of death.

My duties include shepherding cause and manner of death
appeals through the OCME and writing letters with the medical
examiner's response.

The deadline for filing such a request is sixty days after a case
is unpended, but we never paid attention to that. Fowler was
willing to reconsider a determination no matter how much time
passed before the request was made. It's important for the record
to be correct. If something was overlooked or unknown at the
time of the investigation, the medical examiner should know
about it.

The interested person must present new evidence that was
unknown or unavailable to the medical examiner at the time of the
investigation. They can't just ask to reconsider the findings. A
review of the same evidence will lead to the same conclusions, and
that's just a waste of time. There has to be a new fact, a document
or record found, some development meriting reconsideration.

Suicides are disputed more often than any other type of death. Understandably, suicide carries a lot of baggage. Family members wonder whether they should have picked up on self-destructive behavior, whether anything could have been done to prevent a death. The cause and manner of death become part of an individual's legacy. Suicide has undertones of shame, disgrace, and guilt. An accidental death is more understandable and ultimately more acceptable, a fluke of random chance rather than an intentional act.

Several times a year I receive calls from family members concerned about a relative dying in hospice care. Deaths in health care facilities can be medical examiner cases if an injury or some other non-natural factor was involved. Patients do sometimes fall and suffer serious injuries, or they may be assaulted by staff or another patient, or they die unexpectedly during a procedure. These deaths are all investigated by the OCME.

But some people are unclear on the concept of hospice, and are upset to learn after the fact that the elderly family matriarch was killed by an intentional drug overdose given by a hospice nurse. It's murder, they insist. I may get a call from such a person and, upon review of the information, read that Grandma was ninety-six years old and had dementia, diabetes, kidney disease, and end-stage heart failure. It is then my job to explain, in my deep, comforting funeral director voice, that she had a good, long life and was suffering from a terminal illness. The purpose of hospice is to care for people as they die. They didn't kill her, they administered drugs in dosages that were appropriate for hospice care in order to ease Grandma's discomfort. I'm so sorry for your loss, but it isn't a homicide. The OCME will not do an investigation.

Over the years I have written thousands of news stories. My work has made it above the fold. I wrote cover stories for magazines, covered elections and natural disasters. But the most meaningful writing I've done professionally has been for an audience of one or two people — the recipients of letters from Fowler explaining why the manner of death won't be changed. These letters required intense thought and careful use of language.

Writing letters for Fowler gave me an opportunity to smooth his edges. Fowler tends to be very direct in his writing, which can come across as brusque. *"Your request is denied."* It's clear and to the point, but also sounds cold and heartless. Perhaps that's expected from a bureaucrat, but I felt there was a better way. It's possible to be clear and unambiguous while still expressing compassion and relating on a human level. A bureaucrat with heart. If I can't take away the sting of the medical examiner's answer entirely, I can soften it a little.

A young researcher in a neuroscience PhD program at the prestigious Johns Hopkins School of Medicine jumped to his death from a streetlight. Late at night on the medical center campus, he climbed twenty-five feet up a streetlight and dove off. Sad and inexplicable. His parents wrote Fowler asking that the manner of death be changed from suicide to accident. Their son, they said, was obviously in a mental health crisis. I knew the request would be denied and turned Fowler's response into a tribute to their son.

> In the case of your son's death, the incident was witnessed. Bystanders tried to coax him down from the light post. The incident was a deliberate act, which falls squarely within the definition of suicide as a "self-inflicted act committed to do self harm or the death of one's self" in the manner of death classification guide promulgated by the National Association of Medical Examiners.
>
> It may well be that [he] was suffering from some mental disorder. One could argue that most, if not all,

people who take their lives are probably suffering from depression or some other psychological disorder. But even so, this does not change the fact that this was a deliberate, purposeful act done by [him] alone. This is the very definition of suicide, and cannot be categorized as accident or any other manner of death.

I am certain that as a scientist, your son would appreciate that we are obligated to follow evidence no matter where it leads. We must consider facts dispassionately, and not let our personal feelings or beliefs shade our judgement. I believe that this is our way of honoring [him], by remaining true to the scientific principles that he embraced.

Your son's legacy remains intact. His death in no way diminishes what he accomplished in life. From what I gather, [he] was a brilliant and gifted young man. In our hearts, he always will be.

April 18, 2017

In order to measure drugs in the bloodstream, laboratory instruments need to be calibrated with a reference sample of a known concentration. The OCME lab had standardized reference samples for all of the drugs it tested, except for the emerging fentanyl analog carfentanil. To add carfentanil to the lab's testing repertoire, the OCME obtained a small sample of the pure drug — a pinch of white crystalline powder in a glass ampule.

The laboratory had to make a solution of carfentanil by dissolving the drug in liquid. The moment of greatest danger was when the glass ampule was cracked open. It contained enough carfentanil, if dispersed, to kill everybody in the building.

Once the drug was in solution, the danger had passed. Extraordinary precautions were taken to make sure nothing bad happened.

Lab personnel wore head-to-toe protective gear, affectionately called bunny suits, N95 respirator masks and face shields, gloves taped at the wrists. Members of the Baltimore City Fire Department hazmat team stood by in the tox lab, suited up and ready to go. The OCME's ventilation system was shut down during the procedure.

In the IT office, Brian Tannenbaum and I watched video from the ceiling-mounted security cameras in the toxicology department's secured narcotic room. The entire building seemed to come to a momentary halt, as though collectively holding our breath. The bunny-suited techs looked like workers at a nuclear fuel plant, carefully handling the material.

Within minutes the task was done. The ventilation came back on, and the day returned to normal.

The experience made me think. Forensic investigators have told me about going to scenes and finding people with their face planted on a pile of powder. Sometimes powder is on their clothing when they are brought to the OCME.

I asked Fowler whether it would be prudent for the OCME to have Narcan on hand, the drug that reverses the effects of opiates. He said that having one or two doses of Narcan is of little help with powerful drugs like fentanyl and its analogs. Once Narcan is depleted in the bloodstream, the person will slump back into unconsciousness. Multiple doses of Narcan are necessary to counteract fentanyl. We're better off calling 911. An ambulance can be at the OCME in minutes.

"What would we do if somebody here was exposed to fentanyl?" I asked Fowler.

"You're an EMT," Fowler asked.

"I was, a long time ago. I let my certifications lapse years ago."

"You're still an EMT," Fowler said. "You don't forget what you learned. You know how to open an airway and do rescue breathing?"

"Yes sir," I said. "Of course."

"There you go," he said. "Do rescue breathing until EMS gets here."

Within weeks, bag mask ventilators were mounted in the hallway on each floor of the OCME, next to the fire extinguishers and automated defibrillators.

The opioid epidemic, fueled by fentanyl and its potent analogs such as carfentanil, soared unabated. The OCME investigated 1,958 narcotic deaths in 2017, accounting for more than 80 percent of all 2,386 drug and alcohol deaths in the state.

Alarmingly, opioid deaths more than doubled in two years. At this rate of annual increase, within a couple of years the opioid deaths would equal all of the other autopsy cases combined.

Opioid deaths are among the most pathetic and undignified. Once the drug reaches a lethal level in the bloodstream, the user goes to ground like a marionette with its strings cut. Dropped on the spot as though the power were switched off, limbs folded like a rag doll.

For "Porky" Candeloro, that spot was along the train tracks next to I-95 in Morrell Park, a community in the southwest part of the city. He died there on April 4, about two blocks away from my friend Dale Thieler's house.

"Damn shame about Porky," Thieler said when I spoke with him. "He was on his way over here."

I didn't say anything to Thieler about the circumstances of Candeloro's death. The case was still under investigation at the time. Toxicology hadn't even been completed yet. Although I suspected his death was a drug intoxication, for all I knew he could have had a heart attack. It's dangerous to make assumptions just because drugs are present.

But no. Toxicology testing found that Candeloro consumed a powerful mixture of heroin, fenatanyl, and the synthetic opioid U-47700, a toxic cocktail with the enticing street name of "gray death." By the time the tox results came back, I'd moved on. I don't recall ever asking Dale if he knew of Porky's narcotic habit.

Before the year was out, the OCME conducted more than fifteen thousand investigations — a 50 percent increase since I'd joined the agency five years prior. Baltimore had 343 homicides in 2017, the third consecutive year with more than 300 homicides, earning the city the dubious distinction of having the highest per-capita murder rate in the United States.

One more medical examiner was hired during the year. Dr. Nikki Mourtzinos was lured from the medical examiner office in Washington, DC. She is a competent and energetic forensic pathologist who had been involved in the investigation of the 2013 mass shooting in which twelve people were fatally shot at the Naval Sea Systems Command in Washington, along with many other high-profile cases.

With 5,852 autopsies conducted at the OCME that year, one additional forensic pathologist did little to ease the caseload burden. The OCME's medical examiners averaged 385 cases — far above the limit for NAME accreditation. Many of the doctors did more than 450 cases annually.

Despite actively recruiting for the OCME's open medical examiner positions, no other qualified candidates took the bait.

"We're going to lose accreditation," Fowler confided to me, out of earshot, as we walked together to the fourth-floor reception desk to greet a group of pathology graduate students.

Dennis Schrader, the acting Maryland secretary of health, was sympathetic to the OCME's plight. Although educated as an engineer, Schrader had an extensive public health background. He allocated three forensic pathologist positions to hire, if they could be found.

In the meantime, to stave off the risk of losing accreditation, Schrader authorized hiring per-diem medical examiners — doctors paid by the day as contractors to pick up some of the OCME's caseload. Money to pay for the per-diem medical examiners would come from a different Department of Health account, outside of the OCME's budgeted appropriation.

Fowler cultivated a stable of five good pathologists willing to work on a per-diem basis. The per diems were former fellows and pathologists from nearby jurisdictions who commuted in for a day or two. They all had full-time jobs, with the OCME being a part-time side gig for them.

Hiring per-diem medical examiners was a costly and less-than-ideal solution for preserving accreditation. Because they were employed full-time elsewhere, they were mostly available only on weekends.

To avoid disrupting their full-time jobs and paying them another daily rate to testify in court, the per diems tended to be assigned cases unlikely to be criminal matters, such as natural causes and slam-dunk suicides. Simple, straightforward cases. As a result, the burden of the homicides and more complex cases shifted more onto the remaining on-staff medical examiners.

Homicide cases are a huge time suck. Each homicide represents a considerable amount of work after the autopsy. Being subpoenaed as a witness in court means taking a day to review the case file to refresh your memory and understanding of the facts of the case, and at least another day out of the office to testify in court.

Because the OCME has one centralized office where all the medical examiners are based, doctors must travel two hours or more to counties in Western Maryland, Southern Maryland, or the Eastern Shore, where the trials are held. Often, they aren't called to testify as expected and have to return again the next day.

Each of the OCME's medical examiners handles fifty or more homicides every year, compared with five to ten homicides done by MEs in other jurisdictions. Every one of the OCME's medical examiners handles more homicides than any homicide detective in Maryland. The Baltimore City Police Department has more than forty homicide detectives, while the OCME has a third as many medical examiners covering the entire state.

During fellowships, a greater volume and variety of cases provides a better training experience for the doctor. At a training site like New York City's OCME, with five or six doctors in fellowship training, the city's low murder rate means they don't get a lot of hands-on experience with homicides. That isn't an issue at the OCME of Maryland, where fellows can expect to perform 225 to 250 full autopsies during their year of training, including up to 70 homicides.

And now the number of criminal prosecutions involving medical examiners is increasing. State and federal prosecutors have begun going after dealers for fentanyl deaths, charging them with negligent homicide or manslaughter. More criminal cases means more subpoenas for records to use as evidence and more time consumed as medical examiners testify in cases throughout Maryland.

The workload situation was untenable and getting worse. I didn't see how the situation could be resolved without drastic change.

On Memorial Day weekend, my wife and I began watching *The Keepers*, a seven-part documentary on Netflix about the unsolved 1969 murder of Cathy Cesnik, a nun and beloved English teacher at the all-girls Archbishop Keough High School in Baltimore. Some believe her death is related to the alleged sexual abuse committed by the school's priest and counselor, A. Joseph Maskell.

Like the *Serial* podcast about Hae Min Lee's murder, which was also a national and international sensation, *The Keepers* was eerily close to home. Archbishop Keough High School is across the street from St. Agnes Hospital, where my wife worked. The apartment where Cesnik had lived is about half a mile from our home, down Frederick Road near where the buses crashed the year before. The shopping center where Cesnik was last seen alive is another familiar neighborhood landmark.

Werner Spitz, the OCME medical examiner who conducted Cesnik's autopsy in 1969, appears in *The Keepers*, as does Baltimore County homicide detective Gary Childs, whom I know from the OCME's annual homicide seminar. The documentary itself is based on the reporting of former *Baltimore Sun* writers Bob Erlandson and Tom Nugent — the man who introduced me to journalism. *The Keepers* was Smalltimore writ large.

My wife and I were spellbound by *The Keepers*. The Cesnik case is still an active subject of investigation and discussion on social media. As soon as I finished the first episode, I sent an email to the OCME's records department asking them to retrieve Cesnik's case file from the state archives in Annapolis. When the faded gray folder arrived, I secured it next to Hae Min Lee's case file in my desk for safekeeping.

Brian Tannenbaum texted as I was getting ready for work in the morning. "Come to my office when you get here," he said. "You have to see something."

Tannenbaum showed me a video of David Rahim, one of the autopsy technicians, exiting the parking garage across Poppleton Street at around six thirty in the morning. He didn't take more than a step or two out of the door when three black SUVs pulled to the curb. Half a dozen federal agents dressed in black tactical gear jumped out, swarmed Rahim and put him in handcuffs, and hustled him away.

Oh shit.

Rahim, forty-one years old, was a quiet guy. His posts on Facebook were often of a spiritual or religious nature. Nothing about Rahim suggested a proclivity for felony.

A member of the GTTF, Baltimore City police detective Jemell Rayam, a cousin of Rahim, had recruited him for an ill-conceived scheme to rob business owners of $20,000 at gunpoint.

On June 27, 2014, Rayam and other GTTF cops served a search warrant on a store in Southwest Baltimore owned by Jeffrey Shore and Donna Curry. The married couple's store sells pigeons, birdseed, and related supplies. Nothing was seized during the search. One of the cops asked whether the couple had any large amounts of money on the premises. Curry admitted that she had $20,000 in her purse. The money had been legally acquired and was earmarked for paying taxes the next day. Eventually, the cops left empty-handed.

Rayam looked up Curry and Shore's residential address in a law enforcement database. He contacted Rahim and another man from Pennsylvania, Thomas Finnegan, whom Rayam knew was in need of cash. The three cased Shore and Curry's residence and returned shortly after midnight that evening. Rayam gave Thompson and Rahim police uniforms, body armor, and weapons. The cop parked on the street to intercept any police who might respond to the crime while Thompson and Rahim went to the door of the residence. They disabled the security camera and knocked on the front door. When Shore and Curry answered, Rahim and Thompson presented themselves as police and seized the $20,000 in cash.

This wasn't Rahim's first robbery. According to the US attorney, Rahim had perpetrated at least two other residential robberies.

Talk about having a secret life.

The presence of a compromised person in the autopsy room has disturbing implications. There are all sorts of vulnerabilities. Was anything ever stolen from decedents? Could Rahim have tampered with evidence, switched a projectile in a homicide case? I don't know. There was never a review of cases Rahim attended as an autopsy tech.

Rahim got five years in federal prison for his GTTF dalliance.

One of the more enjoyable parts of my job was conducting tours of the OCME. High school students were often the most fun. Nobody under the age of eighteen is allowed in the autopsy area, so high school students don't see any autopsies, bodies, body bags, tissue, or anything remotely disturbing. It's still a very good field trip, with a presentation and a tour of the OCME's laboratories, the Scarpetta House forensic investigator training facility, and the Nutshell Studies of Unexplained Death.

Over the summer, a forensic science student group of the National Honor Society visited the OCME as part of the organization's national meeting in Washington, DC. The large contingent filled the fourth-floor conference room to capacity, about ninety or so people with chaperones. They settled into the conference room with nervous energy, not knowing what to expect. We talked about popular forensic science television shows and all the ways they are inaccurate. I explained why the OCME exists and how it operates.

"There are more than ninety people in this room right now, a random sampling of high school students from throughout the United States, right?" I said to the group. "Do the math. Statistically, about 80 percent of the people in this room will die from natural illness or disease while attended by health professionals. That leaves maybe eighteen people who will die suddenly and unexpectedly. Around two-thirds of these sudden deaths, eleven individuals, will turn out to be due to cardiovascular disease and other natural causes. That leaves seven people.

"Seven people in this room. Statistics suggest that three of these people will die from trauma, some type of accidental death

— a car crash, fall, drowning, or work-related injury. Two will die from an alcohol or drug intoxication. Probably an opioid. One person in this room will be the victim of a homicide. And one person will take his or her own life."

The students looked around at one another.

"Each of us, our days are numbered," I said. "We don't know when that number is up. One day you'll get a phone call and be told that somebody you love is dead. Somebody you know will step out the door to go to work or the store, and they'll never come home again. You'll never speak with this person again. One day, you'll have the last conversation you'll ever have with this person you hold dear. Whatever unfinished business you had will remain unfinished forever.

"Think about the last thing you said to somebody. Was it something said out of frustration or anger? How would you feel about that being your last conversation?

"I've made a conscious effort to try to make sure the last thing I ever say to my wife and children is 'I love you.' What a comforting thought, to leave a memory of my affection for them. It's a little challenging. You never know when a heart attack or stroke will happen. That's the thing about sudden death: It's sudden. So I have to say 'I love you' a lot and hug them often because you never know, one day I might get the last conversation right.

"Every one of us, as long as we are still breathing, has the opportunity to decide what the last conversations will be with the ones we love. Parents and grandparents won't be around forever. If you've been thinking about somebody, missing somebody, haven't talked to somebody in a while, you have the chance to fix that today. Let them know how you feel. Talk as though it could be your last conversation."

As I headed back to my office with my lunch of a hamburger and french fries from the nearby Silver Moon Diner, the elevator stopped on the second floor. King stepped into a car filled with the aroma of warm grease. He was carrying papers and looked harried.

"Are you sure you should be eating that, with your hypercholesterolemia?" he said.

"Some doctor you are," I said. "All of your patients died. I should listen to your advice?"

"Okay, you got me there," he said.

My lunch was interrupted by a call from Andrew Metcalf, a reporter with *Bethesda Magazine.* Metcalf and I worked together at *Patch.* He's a solid, capable reporter, and we always had a collegial relationship.

That morning, a mutilated body had been discovered in a park in Montgomery County, a Washington suburb where the notoriously violent gang MS-13 was active. The Wheaton Regional Park murder was vicious, an act of savagery that would be over the top in a horror film. In the spring of that year, the victim had been lured to the park by a group of MS-13 members and stabbed more than a hundred times. Then his heart was cut out. He was decapitated and buried in a grave that had already been dug in a wooded area.

Months later, one of those present at the murder was in police custody and led them to the grave. Police were digging up the body that morning. A forensic investigator and William Rodriguez, the forensic anthropologist, were at the scene.

"I heard that a body was found at Wheaton Regional Park today," he told me. "Can you confirm that for me?"

I knew that there was an active manhunt for some extremely violent and dangerous people. Any sort of hint that a body had been recovered in the park could tip off the killers. They might eliminate witnesses or evade capture by fleeing the area. I didn't want to give Metcalf any trace of a confirmation. I couldn't keep the information from getting out, of course; he'd get his facts sooner or later. But not from me.

"We don't discuss cases that are under investigation."

"So there is an investigation? Are you confirming that?"

"No, I'm not confirming anything. We don't discuss investigations."

"Did the medical examiner office receive a body found at Wheaton Regional Park today? I'm not asking for any information about an investigation, just whether or not a body is at the OCME. The medical examiner office keeps a record of bodies that are received. That's a public document."

"The Maryland Public Information Act exempts investigative records. We don't discuss cases that are under investigation, Andrew."

"Come on, this is ridiculous." Metcalf said, his voice rising in frustration. "Did the medical examiner office send personnel, or have personnel, at Wheaton Regional Park today? I'm not asking about an investigation; I'm asking about state employees. That's public."

Atta boy, Andrew. Points for persistence. A lesser reporter would have given up.

"Personnel records are exempt from the MPIA."

"You can't withhold this information," Metcalf yelled. "This is nonsense. There are rumors flying around. People have a right to know what's happening. Let me talk with Dr. Fowler. Put him on the phone."

I looked over. The boss was sitting at his desk in the next room, his door open, listening to my conversation.

This should be good. Irresistible force, meet immovable object. I walked to Fowler's office, put my phone on speaker and set it on his desk.

"Dr. Fowler, Andrew Metcalf of *Bethesda Magazine*," I said.

"Hello, Dr. Fowler, I'm looking for confirmation that a body was found at Wheaton Regional Park today."

"We don't discuss cases that are under investigation," he said. That was the end of that.

"Sorry, Andrew," I said, taking my phone back. "Nice to hear from you otherwise. Be well."

Not long after I began work at the OCME, Fowler told me that Russell Fisher's handwritten notes of his evaluation of John F. Kennedy's injuries, as a member of the four-person Clark Panel commissioned by the US Department of Justice in 1968, were "somewhere in the building." This could be a valuable discovery: previously unpublished material about one of most controversial deaths in American history. I made it my mission to find these documents.

Each floor of the OCME has unfinished space to allow for future growth, open areas with no interior walls and hidden from view behind locked doors. This design allowed the costliest parts of construction — concrete, plumbing, and electrical — to be purchased in 2010 dollars. At some point in the future the OCME can finish the spaces with relatively inexpensive drop ceilings, walls, and carpeting. There is enough unfinished space for offices, laboratories, a third huge autopsy room, and anything the OCME may need for decades to come.

During the move from the old Penn Street building, these unfinished spaces were used to store miscellaneous boxes, records, books, artwork, and various odds and ends. Storage rooms throughout the building were filled with dozens of file cabinets and stacks of boxes. The entire place was the attic from hell. Eventually, most of the hoard will have to be thrown away, but in the meantime, nobody has the time or interest to sift through it. There was no telling what sort of historical material was squirreled away.

When time allowed, I nosed through storage rooms and rooted around boxes and file drawers. I found old photos, ancient teaching models and displays. A lot of old records. But I never found any of Fisher's notes.

One afternoon I got a call from Shirl Walker, a former OCME secretary who used to work for the chief. I asked her about Fisher's old files, whether she had any idea what happened to them. "Smialek discarded a lot of old records," she told me. "He hated clutter. Everything was tossed." Walker said she tried to salvage files for things she thought were important and stashed them in the storage room right outside the chief's suite.

Without prompting, Walker told me about the day Smialek died. Everybody who was working at the OCME has memories of that day. Walker told me that after Smialek's death, she cleared out his office. In a desk drawer, Walker found a handgun. "He did get threats," she said. "I wasn't surprised that he armed himself."

How about that. The soft-spoken Canadian was strapped.

Walker said that the storage room near the chief's suite held some interesting material. "You should look through those files," she said. "You'd be amazed what you'll find in there."

Thoroughly intrigued, I moved the clutter around in the storage room to access a horizontal file cabinet along the farthest wall. I went through the drawers file by file. There were some historical cases, some famous and infamous names, and many files for which the significance was unknown to me.

Stuck between two file folders, I found a lumpy manila envelope. Inside was a cassette tape with a note taped across it that said, SMIALEK'S LAST TAPE. It's the dictation tape Smialek was working on when he died, evidence from the worst day in the OCME's history.

I secured the cassette tape in my office for safekeeping. Did Smialek inadvertently record his own death? I don't know. I never listened to it, and doubt I ever will.

On the afternoon of Wednesday, November 15, 2017, Baltimore City homicide detectives David Bomenka and Sean Suiter were canvassing in Harlem Park, a neglected and notoriously violent neighborhood in West Baltimore. They were looking for a potential witness to a triple homicide, a case for which Suiter was the lead investigator.

Suiter was the senior detective of the two. Married and the father of five children, the forty-five-year-old joined the Baltimore Police Department in 1999 after serving in the US Navy. He had been assigned to the Homicide Unit since early 2016. Bomenka, in his fifth month as a homicide detective, was not Suiter's usual partner, but Suiter had requested that Bomenka accompany him to Harlem Park.

Scouting along Bennett Place in their unmarked Nissan Altima, Suiter told Bomenka that he saw somebody acting suspiciously in a narrow, trash-strewn vacant lot between two buildings — a male wearing a black jacket with white stripes. He did a U-turn and parked the car on Schroeder Street at the corner of Bennett Place.

Suiter stood by the empty lot next to 959 Bennett Place and directed Bomenka to the corner of Schroeder Street, hoping to catch somebody who might slip out the back of the property. They'd held their positions for a few minutes when Suiter unholstered his weapon and ran into the vacant lot. Bomenka, out of view of Suiter, heard his partner yell, "Stop! Stop! Stop! Police!"

Gunshots rang out. Bomenka ran to the empty lot and saw Suiter collapse to the ground, shot through the head.

Bomenka dialed 911 on his cell phone and called in a Signal 13. He unholstered his weapon and scanned the area for a shooter. Bomenka didn't see anybody else in the area, or anybody fleeing. Suiter lay prone, mortally wounded, his police radio still in his left hand and his Glock 9 mm service weapon beneath his body.

Suiter was rushed to Shock Trauma. Bomenka described a possible suspect — a Black male wearing a black jacket with a white stripe — they had seen up the street before the chaos erupted. Police cordoned off a six-block area of Harlem Park and began sifting the area for evidence and witnesses.

The six-block lockdown area encompassed a hundred homes, two businesses, and a church. Cops were posted at each block, alleyway, and corner, with checkpoints at each intersection. For six days, residents were stopped when going to or from their homes and questioned by police. They were required to identify themselves, and their names were run through law enforcement databases. Five residences and four vehicles were searched. Nothing of significance was found.

When Linda Thomas heard that a homicide detective had been shot in the head, she asked Wilson, the liaison officer, who it was. As the OCME's front desk receptionist, she was on friendly terms with every homicide cop in Maryland. But Wilson wouldn't tell her. Thomas learned Suiter's identity the same way as everybody else, from the media.

"When I heard it was him, I thought, 'Oh my goodness,'" Thomas told me. "I loved Sean. When he was new to homicide, I helped him a lot. I couldn't believe he was shot like that."

Suiter survived at Shock Trauma for four days. When he died, the forensic investigation became the responsibility of Dr. Aronica.

During the autopsy, Aronica saw a quarter-inch entrance wound on the right side of Suiter's head, above the ear. The exit wound was on the left side of the head, indicating a slightly front-to-back and upward trajectory.

Police investigators had been misled by doctors at Shock Trauma, who believed that the injury on the left side of Suiter's head was an entrance wound. They were wrong. The shot came not only from the right, but from very close range. At least a portion of the gun barrel had been in contact with Suiter's skull when the fatal shot was fired.

Assuming that Suiter had been shot from the left, police had been searching in the wrong direction for evidence. Once they realized the direction from which Suiter had been shot, a projectile was quickly located in the ground.

Aronica found little else of significance during her examination. Suiter's clothing was dirty, which could suggest a struggle. He had small bruises on his left arm and right thigh, but no injuries to his hands or defensive wounds.

She asked police: Is there any possibility Suiter did this to himself? Absolutely not, she was told. Based on the evidence she had, Aronica classified Suiter's manner of death as a homicide.

One week after Suiter's death, on November 22, Baltimore Police Commissioner Kevin Davis held a press conference. Davis told reporters that there was evidence of a brief but violent struggle. Suiter was found with his police radio in his left hand. Three casings matching Suiter's gun were found at the scene.

"Right now, the evidence that's available to us is indicative of a homicide," Davis said.

During the press conference, Davis dropped two eyebrow-raising pieces of information. Suiter was shot eighteen hours before he was to testify in front of a federal grand jury about an ongoing investigation of GTTF members.

And he was shot with his own gun.

CHAPTER EIGHT

TIPPING POINT

Edward Wilson, the bulge of his service weapon visible beneath his polo shirt, stood at the front of the conference room. The seats were filled with forensic science students from a Baltimore County university. A detective sergeant in the Baltimore City Police Department's Homicide Unit, Wilson is one of the few police officers in the country assigned full-time to a forensic medical center. If he isn't busy fingerprinting in the autopsy suite, Wilson often likes to drop into my tours to tell stories and share his perspectives.

"You find a body on the sidewalk, bleeding from the head, and a baseball bat nearby," he said to the group. "What happened?"

"He was beaten with the baseball bat," one student tentatively asked. "Is that too obvious?"

"Maybe. Maybe not," Wilson said. "Are there any other possible explanations for what you find there on the sidewalk?"

"He could have been playing baseball and somebody shot him," another student said.

"Okay," Wilson said.

"He could have fallen out a window, and the baseball bat just happened to be there by coincidence," another student said.

"Sure," Wilson said. "Anybody else?"

"Could have been walking down the street and had a stroke, and be bleeding from the head from hitting the sidewalk," said another voice in the conference room.

"Any number of things could have happened. The things you find at a crime scene, whether drugs or a weapon or anything else, may or may not be related to a death. As an investigator, you have to keep an open mind and gather all the information that you can. Don't make assumptions. You don't know until you have all the facts."

A body with three gunshot wounds seems like an obvious homicide. But not necessarily. People have been known to shoot themselves multiple times taking their own life, even when shot in the head. Gunshot wounds aren't always immediately fatal. A person can survive for minutes, giving them time to try again. In a homicide, the victim could have been strangled or killed by a blow to the head before being shot.

Things are always clear and definitive on the forensic science dramas. The medical examiner does an autopsy and figures out the cause of death. End of scene.

Real life is often messier and more complicated. An altercation may begin with an argument that leads to shoving and grappling, which escalates to punching with fists. One of the participants may pick up a nearby bottle or hammer and use it as a weapon of opportunity. A victim may be kicked, strangled, stabbed, or shot in any combination. Sometimes, for good measure, the victor of the fight sets the loser on fire. A body may come in with many different injuries. The medical examiner's task is to determine which injuries are superficial, which are serious but not lethal, and which are responsible for causing a person's death.

Deaths are more difficult to figure out when trauma isn't involved. A person is found deceased on their kitchen floor, with no signs of injury or foul play. Anything could have happened; heart attack or stroke, some other acute medical condition, drug intoxication or some other kind of poisoning. The possibilities are limitless. These cases can be the most challenging, requiring the most thorough examination; toxicological testing, looking at tissue slides under a microscope; and consultation with neuropathology and cardiac pathology. Every potential avenue must be considered.

I've heard forensic pathology described as the purest form of medical practice. Medical examiners don't have all the instruments and gadgets that help doctors diagnose patients in the clinical setting; pulse oximetry, electrocardiogram, and various beeping devices. You can't ask questions of the dead. How did you feel before you collapsed? Did you feel pain anywhere? Were you dizzy or light-headed? This would be useful information.

Forensic pathologists rely on what they see (the word *autopsy* means "look for yourself") and what they know. To assist them, they have forensic death investigators gathering information for them from any source available. On the crime dramas, FIs are in the middle of the action, processing evidence in the pursuit of justice. In reality, they spend a lot of time on the phone. FIs talk with next of kin and primary care providers to get a medical history, social history, and other details about the decedent. These days, there is an increasing amount of digital information — security video, text messages, browser history. Devices such as Tasers and automated defibrillators retain recorded data that can be printed out. All of this is acquired for the medical examiner.

One of the most important sources is a medical record, particularly if somebody was in a doctor's care or died under sudden and unexplained circumstances. Ordinarily, requesting a decedent's medical record is routine. COMAR requires all hospitals to designate an agent, usually the head of medical records, to respond to medical examiner requests twenty-four hours a day. Because the medical examiner is the attending physician, he is entitled to the deceased's medical record, just as any patient's medical record follows along when changing providers.

The OCME doesn't need a subpoena or signed permissions to acquire a decedent's medical record. Just ask, and it shall be received. Shorter emergency department records may be sent by fax or email, while more voluminous medical records are shipped on disk or in thick envelopes by express delivery.

That's how it's supposed to work. But sometimes a doctor or health facility is reluctant to provide a document, usually because it is evidence that exposes them to liability — a civil suit or regulatory sanction.

When FIs or secretaries hit a wall in attempts to obtain a record, they'd turn to me. My role gave me the opportunity to exercise my natural-born talent for intimidating indignation.

Dr. John Stash, a tall and lanky medical examiner from Texas, came to me about a problem he was having with a nursing home. An elderly woman with dementia was beaten by a health aide in a nursing home and subsequently died. The nursing home refused to provide a copy of the incident report about the assault. Stash was not willing to sign the death certificate until he had the incident report in the case file, even though he knew what the report said.

"They probably don't want to hand over the incident report because the family is going to file a lawsuit," he told me. "Not my problem. The assault isn't documented until I have that incident report. I need that piece of paper."

When acquiring information from reluctant sources, the tools available to the medical examiner are limited. The OCME can obtain an administrative subpoena for records, but that is a time-consuming process involving the attorney general's office and the secretary of health.

I called the nursing home and spoke with the medical records clerk, who referred me to the facility's administrator. The administrator said that the incident report was "being reviewed." With all the authority I could muster in my voice, I spoke slowly, enunciating each word clearly to let the full weight of what I said sink in.

"You are delaying an official death investigation by the State of Maryland, and possibly a criminal investigation," I told the administrator. "There may be very serious consequences for interfering with a state official carrying out their duties." It was a bluff, but it seemed plausible that such a law is on the books. In any event, it worked. The incident report was faxed over within minutes.

I became the OCME's chief kvetcher, taking satisfaction in twisting arms to get recalcitrant sources to do the right thing. Fowler pointed out to me a provision in the Annotated Code that could be useful. Section 5-312 says that "a medical examiner may administer oaths, take affidavits, and make examinations as to any matter within the medical examiner's jurisdiction."

Administering an oath? That sounded like fun. I could work with that. Something about attesting to facts and signing a document under penalty of perjury has a way of sobering people up.

I used this approach for the first time with an arson investigator with a county fire department in the Washington suburbs. The medical examiner had been waiting for the arson report — which would determine whether a death was an accident or homicide — for almost a year. Everything from the police investigation to the family's life insurance and Social Security benefits had been on hold. Repeated entreaties to the investigator and his supervisor were fruitless.

"We need the arson report on this case," I told the investigator over the phone.

"I'll get it to you by the end of the week," he said.

Get off your ass and do your job. "Not good enough," I told him. "Your report is delaying an official death investigation by the State of Maryland and possibly a criminal investigation. How soon can we get your report?"

"Like I said, by the end of the week," he replied.

"That doesn't work for us," I told him. "Tell you what, we'll take the report verbally under oath in a sworn affidavit. How soon can you get here? If you want, I can have the state police give you a ride right now."

That, too, was a bluff. But it got his attention. I heard him cover the phone and whisper to somebody else in the room, "Can they really do that?"

Apparently, the prospect of riding in a cop car to give an affidavit under oath broke the logjam. He came back to me and said, "Fine, I'll work on it right now."

The arson report was in the medical examiner's hands that afternoon.

In January 2018, Governor Hogan appointed Robert R. Neall as secretary of health. Unlike his predecessor, Neall did not have extensive public health experience. He was a fiscal guy.

A former Anne Arundel County executive and state representative who served on the General Assembly's Spending Affordability Committee, Neall focused on limiting the growth of state government spending. Word was that Neall was Hogan's hatchet man, assigned to rein in the state's costliest department. With an annual operating budget of $4.6 billion, the Department of Health made up 27 percent of Maryland's entire $17.2 billion budget. The Department of Health does not have authority over the chief but still controls the OCME's budget and personnel.

Fran Phillips, formerly the health officer for Anne Arundel County, was appointed deputy secretary for public health services. Although the deputy secretary for public health services does not supervise the chief medical examiner, the secretary or their designee is one of five members of the Postmortem Examiners Commission.

The new Department of Health regime did not bode well for the OCME.

One of the most common requests from the public is to view the dead body of a loved one. Many people seem to believe that visually identifying a body is some sort of legal obligation. It's another one of those crime drama tropes, when the morgue attendant pulls back the sheet so a body can be identified. This doesn't happen in real life.

Viewing a body is the least reliable means of identification. The swelling and disfigurement of injuries may make a person unrecognizable. A witness could intentionally mis-identify a body to cover up a crime, or just be mistaken. Fingerprints, DNA, and dental records are more dependable methods of identification.

And then there is the issue of consent. We are obligated to respect the dignity and privacy of the dead. They have not given permission to be viewed after death, and nobody knows whether they would agree to be seen that way. A dead body looks unnatural and disturbing. Imagine waking up on your worst day, unwashed and hair disheveled, to find people staring at you. Would you want to be seen like that? I wouldn't.

Nonetheless, some people insist on viewing their dead loved one. They show up at the reception desk, pleading and demanding to see the body. I explain that the OCME isn't a good environment for a viewing. There is a sparsely furnished viewing room in the autopsy suite, with a glass window that opens into a small refrigerated room. Sometimes this area is used for an honor guard when a cop or firefighter dies in the line of duty, or Orthodox Jews watch over their dead. Once a body has been released to a funeral home, it will be made more presentable and the family can spend all the time they want with their loved one.

On very rare occasions, a modified viewing is arranged for special circumstances. A long-distance trucker from Chicago was killed on a Maryland expressway while trying to retrieve his baseball cap that had flown across the interstate. He left his wallet in the truck cab. A woman who was traveling with him, somebody he met along the way, didn't know the deceased driver and couldn't identify him. Police made a positive identification, but when his mother arrived in Baltimore, she had some lingering doubts. Maybe her son's wallet was lost or stolen, and the driver who died happened to find it. Maybe her son was still alive, stranded somewhere. Before she went through the expense of flying the body home to Chicago, she wanted to confirm that the body was indeed her son. The medical examiner decided to allow a modified viewing.

Fortunately, her son did not have severe facial injuries. A forensic investigator printed out the identity photo taken when the body was checked in to the OCME, a close shot that only showed the face, and brought it to the mother waiting in the reception area.

"That's him," she sighed.

May 21, 2018

Autopsy supervisor Donnell McCullough called and asked me to meet him in the fourth-floor reception area. When the elevator door opened, more than a dozen members of an extended family were waiting for me.

The family's beloved matriarch, the glue that held them together, had died unexpectedly. She was having a direct cremation, going right to the crematory with no viewing at a funeral home. The family gathered — children and their spouses, grand-children, nieces and nephews — to see her one last time. This was their only opportunity to say good-bye.

McCullough said that the viewing had been approved by the medical examiner and asked me to escort the family downstairs. Give me a few minutes, he said.

As I was talking with the family, I glanced at the television mounted to the corner of the reception area, tuned to local news with the sound off. The caption was enough: BALTIMORE COUNTY POLICE OFFICER KILLED.

I walked the family around the corner into the secured area of the building to use the freight elevator, which could hold all of us. I had some reservations taking them into the autopsy suite. The family included a couple of teenagers and a preteen. I wasn't sure they were prepared to see unfiltered death.

The family crowded into the viewing room. On the other side of the glass, the grandmother looked unexpectedly good. McCullough and an autopsy tech had whipped up their morti-cian skills — closing her mouth and eyes, brushing her hair, applying a thick layer of makeup. The body bag was zipped snugly around her head, her face wrapped in a white cotton towel. She looked as good as an open-casket viewing.

I let the family spend some time in the viewing room. They took turns standing at the window to say good-bye. I felt like an intruder, listening to their stories and remembrances. The gathering turned into an impromptu memorial service as they celebrated her life. Afterward, they thanked me for accommodating them.

The news about the cop was grim. Officer Amy Caprio was responding to a call in the Perry Hall community about a suspi-cious vehicle in the area, a black Jeep Wrangler. She found the Jeep and followed it into a cul-de-sac. The Jeep's driver circled around to face the officer in her patrol car. Caprio exited her vehicle and drew her gun and ordered the driver to exit the Jeep.

The driver opened the door as though to comply with the command but suddenly sped toward Caprio. She was able to shoot once before the Jeep ran her over.

Caprio, twenty-nine years old, is the first female Baltimore County police officer killed in the line of duty.

It turned out that the Jeep, which was stolen, was being driven by fifteen-year-old Darrell Ward while three of his friends were burglarizing a home. All four teenagers were charged with first-degree murder and burglary, and subsequently all pled guilty.

When a police officer or firefighter dies in the line of duty, the news carries solemn images of the funerary procession as it travels up I-83 to the Fallen Heroes section of Dulaney Valley Memorial Gardens, emergency vehicles and flags lining the route.

What the public doesn't see is the somber ritual taking place at the OCME. Police vehicles circle the building, lining up on Poppleton Street. Cops representing departments from throughout the state mill around the sidewalks, along with family members and departmental brass. The hearse and vehicles for ranking command are inside the OCME's garage, out of view from the streets. An honor guard stands at attention as the body is brought out of the elevator and draped with a flag.

Rumbles echo between the buildings as motorcycles roar to life. Two motorcycle cops head out to block intersections as the OCME's roll-up door opens and a procession of vehicles slowly make their way down Poppleton, turn left on Baltimore Street, and fade into the distance.

Until the next one. There will always be a next one.

Jarrod Ramos held a grudge against *The Capital Gazette*, the daily newspaper in Annapolis, ever since an unflattering article about him was published in 2011.

A thirty-eight-year-old computer engineer who worked as an IT contractor at the federal Department of Labor Statistics,

Ramos had been the subject of a story about his harassment and stalking of a female high school classmate he contacted out of the blue on Facebook. In a *Capital Gazette* column by Eric Hartley, titled "Jarrod Wants to Be Your Friend," his victim described a "yearlong nightmare" of vulgar and threatening messages.

Ramos pled guilty to a misdemeanor charge of harassment in July 2011. The judge, noting that the behavior was "rather bizarre," sentenced him to probation and ordered him not to contact the victim.

Ramos felt that the newspaper article was defamatory and one-sided. He created a website to air his grievances with Hartley and *The Capital*. "I certainly did a bad thing," he wrote on his site, "but don't shun me for how it was portrayed by this newspaper."

In 2012, Ramos sued Hartley, the paper's editor, and *The Capital Gazette* for defamation, representing himself in court. The lawsuit was thrown out. Ramos appealed the decision, which was also rejected. "He is aggrieved because the story was sympathetic toward the harassment victim and was not equally understanding of the harassment perpetrator," the appeals judge wrote. "The appellant wanted equal coverage of his side of the story. He wanted a chance to put the victim in a bad light, in order to justify and explain why he did what he did. That, however, is not the function of defamation law."

At around two thirty on the afternoon of June 28, 2018, Ramos went to the *Capital*'s offices with a 12-gauge Mossberg 500 pump-action shotgun and a backpack containing smoke bombs and flash-bang grenades. Entering through a side entrance, Ramos barricaded the newspaper's back exit with a Barracuda, a security device designed to prevent an intruder from opening a door.

Approaching the newspaper's main entrance, Ramos blasted the glass door, walked into the office, and began shooting.

Rebecca Smith, a thirty-four-year-old sales assistant who'd just started working for the paper, was his first victim. Ramos shot her twice at her desk by the front door. Continuing through the newspaper's office, he turned right at a row of desks and encountered Wendi Winters, the paper's sixty-five-year-old community beat reporter, who charged at Ramos with a trash can and yelled, "No!" Ramos shot her, paused to reload his shotgun, and continued his rampage. He shot sixty-one-year-old Gerald Fischman, the editorial page editor and columnist, and fifty-nine-year-old assistant editor Rob Hiaasen. Ramos paused again, then walked toward the back of the office, where he shot fifty-six-year-old sports reporter John McNamara.

Inexplicably, Ramos then stopped shooting and hid under a desk. Police responded to the *Capital* office within minutes and found him. Of the eleven people working at *The Capital Gazette* that day, five were killed by Ramos and two were injured trying to hide or escape.

Reporter Phil Davis, who hid under his desk during the assault, told *The Baltimore Sun* that the newspaper's office looked like a war zone.

"I'm a police reporter. I write about this stuff — not necessarily to this extent, but shootings and death — all the time," Davis said. "But as much as I'm going to try to articulate how traumatizing it is to be hiding under your desk, you don't know until you're there and you feel helpless."

Still traumatized by the attack, *The Capital*'s staff regrouped within hours and published a newspaper the next day reporting on the shooting.

I visited the autopsy suite to pay my respects to my fallen colleagues.

In the spring of 2018, the Baltimore City Police Department asked an independent review board to investigate homicide detective Sean Suiter's death. The seven-member panel comprised law enforcement and criminal justice experts, including two former fellow homicide detectives. None of the members had expertise in forensic pathology or crime scene forensics.

To the surprise of many, the review board concluded that Suiter took his own life. The report released on August 27 detailed several points leading the panel to that conclusion.

In the days preceding his death, Suiter had been avoiding his attorney, who had repeatedly called about the detective's upcoming appearance before a federal grand jury. Although the subject matter of Suiter's testimony is unknown, it was related to the GTTF corruption investigation.

Suiter was involved in a 2010 arrest involving Wayne Jenkins, the head of the GTTF. Jenkins allegedly set Suiter up to find drugs that had been planted on a man who fled from police and crashed his vehicle. Suiter was supposedly oblivious to the scheme. He previously worked with two other members of the GTTF, Detectives Maurice Ward and Momodu Gondo, at the notorious Western District police station. Both pled guilty to federal racketeering charges.

In a trial of GTTF co-conspirators, Gondo testified that he used to steal money with Suiter and other Western District cops. He also accused Suiter of planting heroin in a suspect's car to justify a pursuit that resulted in a crash that killed an elderly driver in another vehicle.

Whatever the subject of his testimony, Suiter didn't want to talk about it. When FBI agents tried to interview him, Suiter refused to cooperate and was served with a federal subpoena. He reportedly asked FBI agents: "Will I lose my job?"

After Suiter ducked into that vacant lot on Bennett Place, Detective Bomenka reported hearing as many as five or six gunshots. Investigators found three spent shell casings at the scene, all of them fired from Suiter's weapon. The fatal bullet was consistent with department-issued ammunition. The board concluded that Bomenka heard the gunshots reverberate between row houses, and that's why he thought that more rounds had been fired.

According to the review board, blood spatter was found on the inside right cuff of Suiter's dress shirt. Suiter's DNA, presumably blood, was also detected inside the barrel of his gun. This suggests his right hand was raised near the entrance wound when the shot was fired, with blood expelled into his shirtsleeve and gun barrel.

It's clear that Suiter did not want to talk to that federal grand jury. Perhaps his testimony would place him and others in jeopardy. But that also could be motivation for someone else to silence him.

Nothing about Suiter's death made sense, either as a homicide or as a suicide. How did the gun end up underneath his body? If Suiter meant Bomenka to think he encountered a suspect in the vacant lot, intending to stage his own suicide as a homicide, why shoot himself with his own weapon? Why fire two shots before shooting himself in the head? Surely an experienced homicide detective could have staged a scene more convincingly.

On the other hand, what sort of harebrained hit job relies on overpowering a cop and killing him with his own gun?

With no leads and no suspects, police adopted the review board's conclusion that Suiter's death was a suicide and closed their investigation.

"What did they think would happen?" Fowler chuckled when the review board report was released. "They'd call it a suicide and the death certificate would be changed? That isn't how it works."

"So it will remain a homicide in the official record?" I asked.

"Dr. Aronica isn't inclined to change the manner of death," Fowler said. "There is no new evidence in the board's report, nothing she didn't know when she worked on the case."

"There's nothing the police can do," I said. "They don't have standing for an appeal because they aren't persons in interest."

"And the law excludes appeals in cases of homicide," Fowler said.

Shortly after Sean Suiter's death, I received a phone call from an administrator with the police and firefighter pension plan. The woman on the phone asked for a copy of his autopsy report.

Insurance companies and pensions often request autopsy reports looking for reasons to deny payouts to beneficiaries — money to pay for funeral expenses, to mitigate the effect of a sudden loss of income on a family, to pay off a mortgage so the family can remain in their home, money to provide college education for the children. Money that the family desperately needs.

In the case of Suiter's wife and children, about $500,000 hung in the balance. The Maryland Department of Public Safety provides a $150,000 payment to families of officers killed in the line of duty, on top of a $350,000 cash payment from the US Department of Justice. But if Suiter's death was a suicide, the family would receive nothing.

Although the Baltimore police have closed the file on Suiter's death, the Baltimore City state's attorney considers it an open investigation. Suiter's death certificate and autopsy report still list the manner of death as homicide.

"I'm sorry, that report can't be released while the case is under investigation," I told her.

"Do you know when it will be released?'

"I have no idea."

"Okay, thank you."

Once a month, as regular as a calendar notification, I received a call from the same woman. We had the same brief conversation, month after month. The answer was always the same. After a couple of years, the phone calls stopped. I don't know the outcome. In October 2020, the City of Baltimore agreed to pay $900,000 to settle a workers' compensation claim filed by Suiter's family.

Fowler described the OCME's dire situation at the annual meeting of the Postmortem Examiners Commission. The agency was on track to exceed 15,600 investigations in 2018, including more than 5,700 autopsies. Opiates, such as fentanyl and its analogs, were responsible for 2,128 deaths during the year, accounting for 84 percent of all drug and alcohol intoxication fatalities.

The caseload per medical examiner had gone through the roof. Even with the most favorable math, the average number of autopsies per doctor hit 347 — a Phase II violation that risked the OCME being downgraded to provisional accreditation by the National Association of Medical Examiners.

In reality, the medical examiners were performing well over four hundred autopsies. This made it difficult to recruit forensic pathologists to the OCME, because they could make more money for less work in other forensic medical centers. "Recruiting is difficult," Fowler told the five members of the commission. "The big problem now is that the caseload is scaring people away."

The OCME had to hire two more medical examiners by May 2019, when NAME inspectors would do their next site visit for accreditation, in order to get the caseload average within acceptable limits.

"We need to have two additional MEs on staff, assuming that the OCME doesn't lose any more medical examiners," Fowler said. "That is the real danger right now. If we lose anybody on the existing staff, that puts us into a very difficult situation and likely to result in loss of accreditation."

The OCME's medical examiners were complaining about the workload. Three medical examiners were interviewing for jobs elsewhere, and four medical examiners would be eligible for retirement within the next two years. The OCME was overstretched, about to come apart at the seams.

CHAPTER NINE

GOING TO GROUND

"I have a weird question."

That's what I do, answer weird questions. People call to find out about donating a body to science, "green" burials without embalming or casket, obtaining a blood sample for paternity testing. More than once I've been asked if it's possible to get a sperm sample (it isn't) in order to bear the decedent's baby after his death (which raises all sorts of legal and ethical issues).

I got a crash course on burial at sea. I thought burial at sea was an archaic rite from the days of privateers. It never occurred to me that it was actually still a thing. Burial at sea is perfectly legal as long as the body is dumped three or more nautical miles offshore in water at least six hundred feet deep. Charter boats on the Eastern Shore offer sea burial packages ranging from an intimate ceremony for two in a bowrider up to a catered affair for dozens of mourners on a luxury yacht. The same federal law applies to scattering ashes on water. Scattering must be at least three nautical miles offshore, although there is no depth requirement. But if a person went to Ocean City and discreetly sprinkled ashes into the surf, nobody would be the wiser. No state laws restrict scattering ashes on land in Maryland.

A woman inquired about her sister, more specifically a tattoo on her sister's back. Aside from being a work of art, the tattoo was deeply meaningful to the deceased woman, who wanted it preserved in the event of her death, her sister told me. The family was having a direct cremation, with no viewing or visitation at a funeral home. Her time at the OCME was the only opportunity to harvest the skin with the tattoo. The sister told me that she found somebody who would preserve the tattoo if the medical examiner would only remove the skin from the deceased back. She asked, can that be done?

"The short answer is no," I told her. "The long answer is noooo."

Stripping the skin from the back of a dead body raises all sorts of issues. The OCME is only authorized to conduct forensic autopsies to determine cause and manner of death. We can't do elective procedures. The deceased woman still had rights, even in death, and hadn't legally consented to having her tattoo removed. It can't be done based on secondhand permission. So no, that wasn't going to happen at the OCME.

Speaking with a loquacious drawl, a man called to explain that he was born and raised in Cajun country and only residing in Maryland by happenstance. He'd made arrangements with Louisiana State University to donate his body to medical science and wanted to be sure, should he die unexpectedly, he would be shipped directly to Baton Rouge without a detour through the OCME.

"LSU won't accept a body if it's been cut open for an autopsy," he told me. "I want assurance that my wishes are carried out should I expire in Maryland."

"Well, if you die suddenly and unexpectedly in Maryland, the OCME is required to investigate," I said.

"I don't want an autopsy," he said. "I want to be able to donate my body to LSU."

"Whether an autopsy is done depends on the circumstances," I told him. "If it's a criminal matter, there is no choice. A full autopsy has to be done."

"My wife has power of attorney," he said. "She can speak for me."

"Power of attorney terminates at death," I said.

"It's all spelled out in my will," he said. "All of my kin know that my body is supposed to go to LSU."

"The State of Maryland isn't a party to your will," I said. "The OCME operates under the laws of Maryland."

"Well, what can I do?" he asked.

"If you don't want to come through here, figure out a way to die in Louisiana under the care of a doctor."

In one of the unfinished storage areas on the fifth floor there was a tall dark-green cabinet with small drawers like a card catalog, each with morbid labels: GUNSHOT WOUNDS; LACERATIONS; DROWNING; INFANT DEATHS. The drawers were full of lantern slides, three-by-four-inch plates of glass that were the precursor to Kodak slides, thousands of forensic pathology images collected over half a century. Cataloging and digitizing the collection would be a good project for a graduate student someday.

Browsing through the drawers, holding slides up to the light, I found an image that looked familiar. It was Dealey Plaza. I found four more lantern slides, two that illustrated Kennedy's ballistic injuries and two images that showed the 6.5 × 52 mm cartridges fired from Lee Harvey Oswald's Mannlicher-Carcano rifle. These are the lantern slides that Russell Fisher used for presentations about his Clark Panel work.

Excited about the discovery, I headed back to my office with the treasured artifacts. I ran into Bill Rodriguez, the forensic anthropologist. "Check this out," I said to him, handing him the slides.

He looked at each image. "Pretty cool," he said. "Stay right here. Let me show you something."

Rodriguez walked back to his office and returned with a stoppered glass test tube. In the tube was a single round of 6.5 × 52 mm rifle ammunition. He pulled the stopper and placed the cartridge in my hand.

"This is one of Oswald's bullets," he told me. "It came from a box of ammo that the FBI found searching his apartment. A good friend with the Secret Service gave it to me."

I looked at the slender metallic object in my hand. It felt as though I were touching history.

People presume that a medical examiner office is a dismal place to work. It doesn't have to be. Staff find creative ways to humanize the agency. On most days, there are bowls of candy or platters of baked goods to be found around the building. Ripple has an impressive collection of antique medical and mortuary artifacts in her office. Coriann Self, a secretary who used to be a forensic investigator, has a wall full of photos of her pug in her fifth-floor cubicle and decorative cupcakes hanging from the ceiling. She also collects conjoined and mutant animal crackers for no particular reason. As a gift to Coriann, I offered to preserve the mutant animal crackers and mount them with pins in a shadow box, like a collection of insects.

The Investigations department keeps a Christmas tree decorated for whatever holiday is coming up, so it also serves as a Valentine's Day tree and a St. Patrick's Day tree. Halloween is one time of the year that the OCME lets its hair down. Skeletons and other creepy decorations festoon doors and walls throughout the building. Rodriguez set up a haunted house in an unused room across from the records department. He has an enviable collection of Halloween animatronics, including a simulated electric chair and devices that produce spooky lights and sounds. Only a few outsiders knew about and visited the forensic anthropologist's haunted house at the medical examiner office. Rodriguez also delivers a Halloween lecture on one of his research interests: vampires. It's a solid academic presentation on his work in Romania studying death practices and the origins of vampire mythology.

Fowler authorized me to do anything that enhanced morale at the OCME. I was put in charge of having plaques made when employees retired — in the shape of Maryland with the OCME's seal — and adding framed photos to the fifth-floor rogue's gallery when new medical examiners were hired, pushing Quincy's photo a little farther down each time.

I organized lunchtime walks to the historic Davidge Hall at Lombard and Greene and to Edgar Allan Poe's grave. Fowler let me charge $900 to his personal credit card to buy pizza for the entire staff. Brian Tannenbaum, Mike Eagle, and I organized a chicken soup contest, with each of us cooking our version of the matzo ball classic (I came in third). Anything involving free food is popular with OCME staff, so the event was followed up with a chili cooking contest.

A few civilian employees of the Baltimore City Police Department crime lab visited the OCME to see the Nutshell Studies of Unexplained Death. They returned the favor by hosting a group from the OCME to tour the police crime lab. A large group of us, including several medical examiners and tox lab scientists, walked down Baltimore Street to police headquarters to learn about fingerprinting and see the trace evidence lab and ballistics unit. It was a useful experience for each organization to learn more about how the other operates.

One of the tours I conducted through the OCME included Sally McMillan Robb, an attorney who is active in Chesapeake Search Dogs, a volunteer organization that does K9 search and rescue operations. Police, fire, and rescue agencies throughout the region call upon Chesapeake Search Dogs to track lost persons, find victims in structural collapses, and search for dead bodies.

After her tour, Robb contacted me with an unusual request. Chesapeake Search Dogs trains their animals for cadaver search with scraps of clothing from dead bodies, material kept from old cases they have worked. All they had left were a few old shirts tattered to shreds by enthusiastic puppies thinking they were playing a game. Cadaver-scented fabric isn't something you can buy on Amazon. Robb asked whether there was any way the group could acquire a fresh supply of cadaver material.

Need dead body juice? I'm the guy.

I went to the autopsy suite to talk with Ricardo Diggs, the Ambassador of Decomp. The OCME goes through white cotton terry-cloth towels by the case. These towels are used to mop up fluids, stuff into body cavities after the autopsy, and a variety of other purposes, then thrown away rather than laundered. They are perfect for cadaver samples: clean, durable, and standardized. Diggs agreed to place towels beneath decomposing bodies, let them dry out, fold them, and seal them in individual gallon-sized Ziploc bags.

We could give Chesapeake Search Dogs a set of ideal cadaver reference samples for search dog training, dozens of towels from different bodies in different stages of decomposition, at no cost to the organization. Just another public service provided by the State of Maryland.

I had been playing telephone tag with Robb to discuss the logistics of how the bags prepared by Diggs would be collected and handed over to Chesapeake Search Dogs. We finally had a chance to talk on the phone while I rode a Lyft home from work. A lot of work-related conversations are too distasteful for the general public, but this one topped them all.

I don't know how much the Lyft driver paid attention to my conversation. I'm sure he heard enough. We made eye contact in the rearview mirror a couple of times during the ride. It was clear I was talking about decomposing dead bodies with somebody who shared that interest.

As Robb and I talked about collecting and preserving decomp fluid, the Lyft driver was being dumped by his girlfriend via text messages. The driver had his phone mounted on the dashboard so he could follow the route on the map. A text window kept popping up. He replied to her texts while stopped at traffic lights. Because the screen was right in front of me, I read along with him. I watched the driver's world implode before my eyes during the ride home.

> I've had it with you. We're over.
>
> baby please
>
> we're done. i don't want you around anymore.
>
> we'll talk later
>
> done talking. get your stuff out of my place.
>
> baby please
>
> don't baby me. i'm not your baby. you got 24 hours or it's going in the dumpster.

He was having a very bad evening. It was brutal. I felt bad about reading his texts, but not really. He could have moved the phone, or ideally ignored the phone and paid full attention to driving until my ride was over. He chose to display his immolation in front of me. Meanwhile, I was in back talking explicitly about decomposing bodies, disgusting fluids and smells. We were both engaged in indecent conversations with an absolute lack of consideration for the other occupant of the vehicle.

After stepping out of the car, I'm sure the Lyft driver had the same thought I did: *That's the weirdest fucking ride I've ever had in my life.*

The canine members of Chesapeake Search Dogs perform double duty. Aside from searching for the lost and the dead, the animals are trained therapy dogs often taken to visit patients in hospitals and nursing homes. Being petted and praised is therapeutic for the animals, too. In appreciation for our help providing them with cadaver towels, Robb and two other Chesapeake Rescue Dogs volunteers offered to bring some animals to the OCME for a visit.

Something as simple as having therapy dogs visit the OCME involved a few hurdles, however minimal. Fowler had to approve the visit, which he did. Walking the dogs around the building from office to office was out of the question. Some people may have allergies or be fearful of dogs, he said. Good point. The dogs would be limited to the public area on the fourth floor, and employees could come spend time with them if they chose. The visit should be scheduled for the afternoon, when autopsies are done for the day. Three o'clock was ideal, when Investigations and the tox lab change shifts and the maximum number of people were in the building.

At the appointed time, four of the gentlest and softest dogs were escorted into the Investigations department. Linda Thomas announced the visit throughout the building over the PA system. The room quickly filled with staff — doctors, lab personnel, secretaries, autopsy techs. People sat on the floor, crawled, and frolicked as the dogs wandered from person to person, wagging their tails and placidly soaking in the attention. Staff talked about their own dogs and shared photos. Thomas, wary of dogs, watched from a distance from her seat at the reception desk.

Usually when there is an event involving food, staff tend to cluster together by department, with doctors sitting together, tox lab people with their own clique, autopsy techs in a group. I'd never seen so many OCME staff mix it up and crowd into a room to socialize. All it took was dogs.

"This was the best day ever," one of the medical examiners said as she headed back to her office.

March 27, 2019

Early in the morning, I received a text from Samantha Thieler, Dale's daughter. We remained close as she grew up, married, and moved to the West Coast to raise a family. She still hugs when we see each other.

> my dad is gone
>
> what?
>
> he died.
>
> oh no, sam. i'm so sorry. my heart is broken.
>
> part of me knew he was on borrowed time, and another part thought he might have just been too mean to die.

Sam told me that Dale had been using narcotics. Things had become much worse over the last twelve to eighteen months. Dale always drank a lot, but I didn't realize the extent of his substance abuse. His casual flirtation with opiates and other drugs grew into an addiction that forced him to buy crap from the same streets I drove through every day to work, where corner boys hawk their products.

Sam had grown so alarmed that she considered telling him about Bad Batch Alert, an anonymous texting app developed by a group of Baltimore teens with the support of the Baltimore City Health Department. Bad Batch Alert identifies areas with high rates of overdoses, indicating the presence of strong opiates like fentanyl in the neighborhood. Does the app save lives, she wondered, or tell users where to go to find the good stuff?

I thought back to the last time Dale visited me, just a couple of weeks ago. He'd dropped by unannounced, as he often did. We sat on my back porch and drank coffee. Nothing seemed out of the ordinary. The last thing we talked about was probably the weather, since it was an unseasonably warm spring day. Should I have known? Could I have done something?

When Porky died on the railroad tracks, Dale said he'd been on his way to his house. Was the deadly batch Porky acquired meant to be shared with him? Why didn't I ever wonder this before? In hindsight, it seems obvious. I had no idea about this other part of my good friend's life.

Dale and I spent countless hours talking about Baltimore history, particularly the historic B&O Old Main Line that practically runs through our backyard to Ellicott City. How many hundreds of games of chess did we play over the past four decades? There would be no more talking. No more chess. Never again will I hear the guttural rumble of his motorcycle announce his arrival for a visit.

The next day I saw Dale listed on the morning conference sheet. Dr. Jack Titus would be handling his case. He was in good hands. Titus is well respected as a forensic pathology teacher. He used to head up the fellowship training program. I read the investigator's report at my desk and went to the autopsy suite to pay my respects. By the time I got to the second floor, the examination was well under way. I sat in the gallery and watched Titus work.

"You fucked up real good this time, bud," I muttered to myself.

I always imagined us growing old and gray, a couple of old guys hunting rats in Baltimore's alleys on lawn chairs in Bermuda shorts. That will never happen. I was not prepared for this.

I never thought I'd see the inside of Dale's skull.

Michelle moved in with her sister after Dale's death and had to off-load a lot of the stuff accumulated by a family over a lifetime. One of the items she no longer had room for was the liberated state park picnic table from the yard. The heavy wooden table now occupies my back porch, still a place for convivial gatherings, memorialized with the engraved names of those no longer with us.

My phone rang while I was in the shower one morning. I could see the incoming number on the screen of my phone next to the sink. Somebody was calling me directly, rather than being forwarded from the office, in which case it would display OCME's main number. This can indicate an important call, such as a deputy secretary of health or a state delegate's office doing constituent service. These calls require prompt attention.

I turned off the water and stepped out of the shower, dripping suds onto the bathmat, and answered the phone.

"Hi, Bruce. Harvey Levin with TMZ," said the voice on my phone. "We heard that Lauren Braxton died and we're looking to get confirmation."

"Who?"

"Lauren Braxton," Levin said. "Toni Braxton's niece."

Still no help. I soon learned that Lauren Braxton was some sort of celebrity. Her celebrity family said that Lauren died from a heart condition, but others suspected drugs were involved. What a life I have, getting breaking celebrity news directly from Harvey Levin of TMZ. While naked.

"We don't discuss cases that are under investigation," I said.

Levin explained again about the heart condition and his impending deadline. *Sorry, but your deadline and sense of urgency are not my problem.*

"We don't discuss cases that are under investigation," I repeated. Levin's a persistent guy; this was the third or fourth time we'd spoken about celebrity deaths. The first time while naked.

With Fran Phillips as deputy secretary, the Department of Health wanted more of a hand in responding to media requests involving the OCME, particularly when it came to high-profile or celebrity deaths likely to draw significant press attention.

The majority of press calls are one-off, a reporter wanting to know the identity or cause of death for a body found somewhere. I became adept at giving out as little information as possible. Not a word more than cause and manner of death. A reporter from a local television station called to find out the cause of death of a woman killed in a car crash.

"The cause of death was multiple injuries," I told him.

"Can you tell me what that means?" he asked.

"There was more than one injury," I said.

"Can you tell me more about the injuries?"

"They were fatal," I said.

For a while the Department of Health wanted all press inquiries to be directed through their media office, even for routine
cause and manner of death inquiries. This resulted in a frustrat-
ingly long series of emails back and forth between me and the
Department of Health answering their follow-up questions:
When will the investigation be done? What does "undetermined" mean? When will the autopsy report be available? They
eventually decided to take themselves out of the loop for routine
inquiries but wanted to be notified of high-profile and celebrity
deaths.

But I am not a good judge of celebrity status. My pop-culture
education is woefully inadequate. Lor Scoota, Dee Dave, Biz
Markie, rappers who died in Baltimore during my time at OCME,
were admittedly not within my realm of cultural experience. I
didn't know Carl Ruiz was a Food Network star chef. I found out
who they were real quick, but only after news stories of their
deaths went viral online.

The MDH media office got particularly bent out of shape over
a *New York Times* story about a banker from Connecticut charged
with manslaughter for the death of a handyman at a resort on the
Caribbean island of Anguilla that mentioned Fowler.

According to reports, maintenance worker Kenny Mitchell
arrived to repair a sink at the suite where Gavin Scott Hapgood
and his family were staying. Inexplicably, a fight broke out
almost immediately. Hapgood restrained Mitchell until police
arrived. While Hapgood held him down, the maintenance
worker went unresponsive and died. A coroner ruled that
Mitchell was asphyxiated, and Hapgood was charged with
manslaughter.

At the request of Hapgood's lawyers, Fowler was asked to consult on the case. Fowler pointed out that the maintenance worker had cocaine in his bloodstream at a concentration of twice the level considered lethal and determined that he had died of cocaine intoxication, not asphyxia.

The Department of Health media office expressed their extreme displeasure at being blindsided by a *New York Times* article. Fowler explained to them that the OCME has no control over whether information is presented in a criminal trial, as in this instance, or released by a police department. We didn't know about its release until it appeared in print.

One Friday evening in late June, while walking through the ground-floor garage on the way to my car, I saw Dawn Epperson, a forensic investigator, and Dr. Derek Musgrove, a fellow near the end of his training, lugging a large garbage can from the back of one of the OCME's transport vans. A blue tarpaulin had been stuffed into the bin, which was clearly heavy. The garbage can was found in a West Baltimore vacant lot. A passerby detected a strong odor and notified the police.

When a body is found wrapped in a sheet or blanket, or stuffed into a suitcase, the protocol is for everything to be brought into the OCME intact so it can be opened and documented under controlled conditions. The body is carefully unwrapped one layer at a time, so the material can be examined and photographed.

On Saturday morning, the garbage can was taken into one of the biosafety rooms. The medical examiner and autopsy technician thoroughly inspected and photographed the garbage can, then lifted the bundle out and placed it on the autopsy table. The tarpaulin was examined and photographed from all sides then carefully unwrapped, revealing two large heavyweight plastic contractor's trash bags, each knotted closed. Painstakingly, the trash bags were photographed and opened to reveal . . . two hundred pounds of putrid chicken parts that somebody dumped on the city streets.

The meeting of the Postmortem Examiners Commission on November 7, 2019, was unlike any I had seen before. Usually only a small group attends these pro forma meetings — the five members of the commission, Fowler, and me. This time, OCME staffers wanted to speak their minds directly to the commission. More than thirty were present in the conference room, including most of the medical examiners.

Fowler began the meeting with his update of OCME operations. The agency projected having almost sixteen thousand investigations in 2019 — up 60 percent from 2012. Population growth couldn't explain the dramatic rise in caseload. Maryland's population gains about fifty thousand people every year, Fowler said, which should contribute about a hundred additional medical examiner cases annually. The rapid increase was largely due to the opioid epidemic — more than two thousand additional fatalities annually — and the street violence that went along with it, he said.

The OCME was expected to complete more than six thousand autopsies in 2019, up nearly 60 percent from 2012. Each of the medical examiners was performing more than 350 autopsies a year, far beyond the serious Phase II violation limit for National Association of Medical Examiners accreditation. Three medical examiners were doing 400 to 450 autopsies, and three were doing more than 450. One powerhouse doctor performed 490 autopsies, nearly twice the Phase I limit.

"The individual totals of some of these medical examiners clearly violates national practice standards," Fowler said. "I don't know how much more they can bear."

In a 2018 survey of two hundred National Association of Medical Examiners members, the OCME of Maryland ranked top in the nation for caseload per medical examiner. The crushing case-load was making it impossible to recruit medical examiners to the OCME. "This is one of the primary factors we face when trying to recruit," Fowler said. "The caseload scares them off."

The burgeoning caseload threatened the viability of the building itself. Trends prior to 2012 suggested the OCME would not even reach six thousand autopsies per year for many years into the future. The OCME's current building was designed to last forty years, with a maximum capacity of eight thousand autopsies a year. "If cases continue to increase at this rate, we're looking at reaching maximum capacity in ten to twelve years, not forty years," Fowler said.

The Investigations department had experienced an employee turnover rate of 50 percent over the previous eighteen months. Investigators train at the OCME and get a little experience, then jump to another medical examiner office for more money. "We've become something of a training farm," Fowler told the commission. The only way the department could operate was with mandatory overtime, which added to dissatisfaction and burnout.

Fowler's report was sobering. "We're still here," he concluded. "We're still open for business."

Fran Phillips spoke of the OCME's role in the public health system and the importance of timely and accurate mortality data.

"From a public health standpoint, the quality of the science that comes from this office is unparalleled," Phillips said. "It is the backbone of so much of what we are able to do in Maryland in public health, in terms of surveillance and in terms of assessing and calibrating our interventions. The whole area that we're struggling with now, with opioids, has largely been driven by the data and the science that comes from this office."

But in terms of addressing the exigent crisis facing the OCME, Phillips offered no answers. "I don't have solutions for these immediate, pressing staffing and accreditation problems," she said.

Ripple, one of the deputy chiefs, was first to speak for the OCME staff. "If we don't get more MEs, it's not going to be sustainable," she said to the commissioners. "What's going to happen is there will be errors. Bodies have to be held over. Families won't get closure, funerals are delayed, criminal investigations are delayed, evidence gets lost. If you shift cases from one day to the next to the next, we all lose."

Ripple's voice cracked with emotion. "We all want this office to succeed," she said. "It's been one of the best in the country for a long time. There are a lot of offices in the country that were good, went downhill, and crashed. We don't want that to happen, but the way it is now we just can't sustain it."

Next to speak was Aronica, who was in her seventeenth year as medical examiner. "I cannot keep up with the workload," she said. "I've been hanging on for as long as I can."

Aronica told the commission that she was looking for work elsewhere. Other offices were offering medical examiners more money for less work. "This is an amazing place with amazing people," she said. "Everyone here is extremely talented and great to work with, but I can't keep up with the workload."

Titus had brought along a file folder of printed news stories about medical examiner offices across the country that imploded, usually after a series of crises with tragic and avoidable consequences.

"Boston went through it," he said. "New Jersey, Cook County, New Hampshire, Los Angeles County, Virginia, Connecticut, Delaware. I don't want to see what happened to them happen to us."

Ripple stood to elaborate on Titus's point. "One of the best things about this office is that we're not in the news," she said. "We don't want to be those offices that mislabel bodies, or lose bodies. We don't want to make mistakes. We're holding it together — the MEs, autopsy services, Investigations, secretaries, every aspect of this office. We're holding it together, but there is a limit. We don't want to see the first statewide medical examiner system in the United States go down the toilet like all these other places."

Speaking out was cathartic. After the meeting, I felt oddly elated. The message had been loud and clear: The OCME was at imminent risk of collapse. Surely now that the issue was out in the open, something would be done. I thought we had won.

Two weeks after the Postmortem Examiners Commission meeting, Fowler called me into his office when I arrived at work. He handed me a sheet of paper. "Would you review this for me?" he asked. I read the document.

> After much careful thought, I have decided for personal reasons to resign my position as Chief Medical Examiner for the State of Maryland, and retire from state service effective December 31, 2019.

Oh shit.

State officials — the Department of Health and the Department of Budget and Management — were inured to Fowler's dire forecasts. They had heard it all before, and yet the OCME was still able to function as reliably as always. "It was obvious that I'd used up all the credibility I had with the health department," Fowler told me.

The situation had become untenable. He had carried the ball as far as he could, and it was up to somebody else — an outsider — to provide the State of Maryland a cold splash of reality.

The news of Fowler's departure filtered through the building. For most staff, Fowler was the only chief they'd ever known. There was a boding uneasy sense of a life-changing event, a transition into the unknown. It felt a lot like grief.

I found Stash standing in the fifth-floor hallway in front of the gallery of medical examiners who have served at the OCME, sixty men and women representing a continuum back to Maldeis in 1939. We looked at the familiar faces together.

"I wonder what will happen," he said to me. "I worry about an outsider coming in and destroying everything that's been built."

On his last day, Fowler gave me a bottle of South African wine — unwrapped, in brazen violation of state rules. He set the wine down and tapped a can of polyurethane spray amid the clutter on my desk, part of my project to preserve Coriann Self's mutant animal crackers.

"To accompany your huffing," he said.

"Thank you," I said. "It's been a privilege to work for you. I'm not sure why you hired me, but I'm grateful that you did. This has been the experience of a lifetime."

Fowler handed me his box of challenge coins, the ceremonial swag coveted as an enduring symbol of the OCME. "I trust you to take care of these," he said.

The challenge coins were heavy in my hands. "I'll do my best," I said.

I spent time in the afternoon sitting at the reception desk while Linda Thomas was out for a medical appointment. In the lobby was the mother of a twenty-three-year-old man, one of three people shot in a neighborhood dispute. The wounded were at Shock Trauma and may end up here. Baltimore was in a spasm of violence, approaching the all-time record of 353 homicides set in 1993, when the population of the city was one-third larger. In one three-day period before Christmas, there were 18 shootings and 8 homicides.

The twenty-three-year-old's mother asked me for details of the shooting: How many times was he shot? Where on his body? I couldn't disclose that information. She wanted to see him, to see her baby. I'm sorry, we can't allow that, I told her. You can see him at the funeral home. I'm so very sorry for your loss. Bereft, she sat in the lobby and sobbed.

A detective came to the window to get a temporary swipe card allowing him to go to the autopsy area and pick up evidence. He was working a triple homicide. I was reading an online news story about the shooting when he approached.

"Do you have the shooter?" I asked him.

"We thought so, but no. A guy showed up at the Hopkins ER shot through the nose," he said, tapping his finger below the bridge of his nose. "He claimed that he was shot at Fayette and Holliday, right next to police headquarters. We looked at video, and sure enough he was telling the truth."

As 2019 drew to a close, it was difficult to imagine how things could possibly get worse.

— CHAPTER TEN —

DEATH SPIRAL

Things got much worse in 2020. The OCME began hemorrhaging personnel. Within a short period of time six doctors retired or took jobs at other offices, including a deputy chief. Most of them were experienced, senior medical examiners.

The emergence of Covid-19 disrupted the OCME much as it did all organizations. Some staff were allowed to work remotely or were temporarily furloughed. As emergency essential staff, I was required to report to the office every day.

For three months, I was assigned Covid screening duty in the ground-floor garage. I sat in an uncomfortable chair by the roll-up entrance door, asking questions of body transport personnel and delivery drivers. It was cold and very boring.

Sudden deaths due to Covid had only a moderate effect on the OCME's caseload. The vast majority of Covid-related deaths occurred in hospitals, where a person was known to have the illness and was attended by doctors and medical personnel. Because Covid illness is a natural cause of death, these did not meet the criteria for a medical examiner case. However, there were people who didn't have health insurance, didn't go to the doctor, weren't known to be infected with Covid, and died at home with no medical care. On most days, the OCME received at least a few such cases.

Southall was appointed acting chief medical examiner until a permanent chief could be recruited to the OCME. She remained in her corner office on the south side of the building and never occupied the chief's offices. I had the chief's suite to myself, isolated from the rest of the OCME staff. I ate alone at Smialek's table.

Appreciating the quietude, I unwrapped a bacon and egg sandwich from the local carryout and took a bite. A housefly swooped in and landed on my sandwich, right at the notch left by my teeth. My eyes focused from the sandwich to the window on the other side of the table, overlooking the snow-frosted Poppleton Street parking garage. It was freezing outside. There was no insect activity. The fly, recently hatched from a dead body in the autopsy suite, had somehow managed to meander up three stories and find my sandwich. I wrapped up what was left and threw it in the trash.

With court cases postponed due to Covid, there were no subpoenas to track. No tours or in-person visits were allowed in the OCME. There was little for me to do but bide my time. Once in a while there was a phone call or email to respond to, but most of my days were spent hunkered down in the chief's suite with the overhead lights turned off.

Phone calls were a welcome break from the monotony. A woman called looking for her brother, Jerry Baker. "I heard yesterday that he was found dead in a house," she told me.

I searched the CME and found two Jerry Bakers in the database, but none recently. One case was three years old, and the other dated from 1997. I checked the daily conference sheet to see if there was an unknown from Baltimore City. Nothing.

I went back to the results with the two Jerry Bakers and asked the caller for her brother's date of birth. Bingo.

"Ma'am, he died three years ago," I told her.

She began sobbing. "I knew it was true as soon as I heard it," she said. "I knew he was dead. This just hit me."

"The cause of death was . . ."

"Drugs," she interrupted. "I know, it was drugs. I always knew he'd die from a drug overdose."

"No, the cause of death was cardiovascular disease compli-cated by sepsis and morphine and fentanyl intoxication," I said. "The manner of death is undetermined."

"Oh," she said.

Walking through the first-floor garage, my cell phone rang. A man was calling from the lobby of Holy Cross Hospital in Silver Spring, a Washington suburb, with a story about being menaced by a paranormal presence at three o'clock the previous morning. He wanted me to have the security video from the hospital lobby pulled to verify his version of reality. I suspected that he was experiencing auditory hallucinations.

"We don't have the authority to acquire video from Holy Cross Hospital," I told him. "I'm not sure I understand what this has to do with the medical examiner office."

"You guys investigate death, right? If there were a spirit or ghost liberated from a body you would investigate it, right?"

"Excuse me?"

"A paranormal presence. A ghost. That is something you would investigate," he said. "The proof is on the video."

"All we do is determine the cause and manner of death," I said. "The medical examiner's authority ends at death. We don't inves-tigate beyond that."

"But this is related to death," he said.

"We don't investigate paranormal activity."

Click. He hung up.

Who you gonna call? Not the OCME.

For only the fifth time in its eighty-year history, the OCME had a new chief. In early 2021, the Postmortem Examiners Commission appointed Dr. Victor W. Weedn as chief medical examiner. Weedn has an impressive résumé on paper. A Texas native, he is a forensic pathologist and attorney. He received his medical degree from University of Texas Southwestern Medical School and his JD from South Texas College of Law. For a couple of years, Weedn was an assistant medical examiner under Fowler at the OCME. Weedn formerly headed up the New Jersey medical examiner office and was past president of the American Academy of Forensic Sciences. Most recently, Weedn was a professor in the George Washington University forensic science program.

I had known Weedn for several years. He regularly brought his forensic science students to the OCME to observe autopsies. I wasn't sure whether he was the OCME's savior or the sacrificial lamb brought in to reveal unpleasant realities to state budget officials.

As the new chief medical examiner, Weedn's style was markedly different from his predecessors'. Although he had been hired by the Postmortem Examiners Commission to bring the OCME out of crisis, he seemed more interested in establishing his mark than addressing the agency's looming problems.

Weedn's relationship with the medical examiners started out badly when, during his first meeting with the doctors, he reportedly told them their work was terrible, and it deteriorated from there. Most of the pathologists have vastly more experience in the autopsy room than he does.

Friction between Weedn and me began with the gallery of medical examiner photos, the visual history of the OCME. Weedn pointed out that he is the first assistant medical examiner to work elsewhere and return to the OCME. I guess that might be true, I said. I told him I'd make a new label that said 2009–2011, 2021–PRESENT for his head shot. Weedn suggested that maybe he should have a second photo on the wall as chief, in chronological order. Maybe it should also be in color, different from all the others. Fowler didn't have a second photo in the sequence when he was made chief, I said. But he persisted.

What a petty thing. Why are we wasting time talking about a photo?

I changed the label and left it at that, a minor act of insubordination.

In staff meetings, Weedn described ambitious goals: enhancing the investigation of sexual assault by hiring a forensic nurse, assuming the responsibility of fingerprinting and body identification, embarking on research projects. Any of these ideas would be worthy of consideration if the OCME were running on all cylinders. But in its wounded and limping condition, the staff barely keeping it together, it was too much to contemplate. Everybody is rowing the boat as hard as they can, and the boss wants to water-ski. It isn't going to happen.

Within a short period of time, Weedn alienated himself from nearly the entire OCME staff. More medical examiners left the OCME: Mourtzinos, Allan, and another doctor who recently completed her fellowship. The OCME's chief of investigations resigned, a key staff member who trained and supervised a dozen full-time FIs and a network of more than one hundred on-call field investigators throughout the state and maintained the written policies and procedures needed for accreditation on the Google Drive. Brian Tannenbaum decided that he'd had his fill of the OCME shitshow and took a job in the private sector, working remotely from home for more pay. Hard to blame him.

After my father died in 2011, my elderly mother remained in Buffalo for several years. She constantly complained about the weather. Snow. Piles of snow. Freezing temperatures. Slippery sidewalks and black ice on the streets. What do you expect? It's Buffalo.

In 2017, my mother was finally convinced to move to an independent living senior community near my sister's home outside of Jacksonville, Florida. It was a lovely residence, conveniently close to family. Most important, there was no snow. My mother complained about the sunshine instead. It was always sunny and warm. The sun was too bright.

"Do you have to shovel sunlight from the sidewalk?" I asked.

"No," she said. "This isn't so bad, I guess. I'll manage."

She was in pretty good health for a woman in her early nineties. No heart disease, cancer, major illnesses, or mobility issues. She hadn't smoked in decades and rarely drank more than an occasional glass of wine. Her vision and hearing were failing, but other than that she had a clean bill of health. Mother was active and lived independently.

Covid made life difficult at her senior community. Group meals in the dining room were discontinued. Residents had to eat all their meals alone in their apartments. My mother complained about the isolation, the frequent temperature checks, all the rigmarole. There were so many strict rules now. I told her that's a good thing. With news stories of Covid running like wildfire through nursing homes, it was reassuring to know that they were being so diligent where she lived.

They were diligent for a year. Then one evening in January 2021, the facility allowed my mother to share a meal in the dining hall at a table with another resident. Nobody knew it, but the elderly gentleman across the table from her was infected with the Covid-19 virus. My mother was sick within days. She was found unconscious on the floor of her apartment, taken to the hospital, and admitted to intensive care. When nothing more could be done, she was transferred to the hospice unit.

My sister, suited up in protective gear like a member of the hazmat team, was able to visit our mother at the hospital. But travel restrictions prevented her other four children from seeing her before she died of Covid illness on January 23. Helane Laufer Goldfarb was ninety-three years old.

"Don't come to my funeral," my mother often cursed when annoyed. "I don't want you there. If you don't visit me during my lifetime, don't come after my death."

As it turned out, because of travel restrictions, none of her family was able to be present at her funeral. We watched her graveside service on Facebook Live and later held a virtual shiva on Zoom. This is mourning in the age of Covid.

I thought back to the last conversation I had with my mother. We spoke every Sunday morning. In recent years, her diminished hearing and dour mood made communicating difficult. Some weeks our chats were brief and superficial. But the last time we spoke, the Sunday morning before she became ill, my mother was in an ebullient, talkative mood. Mother told stories I've heard many times before, stories about growing up with her beloved older sister. I listened, and we chuckled at the funny parts. We talked for a long time.

It was a good conversation. The last thing she said to me was, "I love you."

Laurel police chief Russ Hamill notified the OCME of a homicide on the afternoon of February 3. He told forensic investigator Anthony McCaffity that the victim was one of our own: Brian Bregman. A well-respected attorney, reserve officer for the DC police, and volunteer firefighter, the forty-three-year-old Bregman was an on-call forensic investigator for the OCME, responding to deaths in Prince George's County.

"When I heard who it was, I thought he might have been killed in traffic or something," McCaffity told me. "Then I heard what happened."

Bregman met a woman, twenty-three-year-old Marie Nancy Hassan, through an online app. On the evening of January 30, he invited Hassan to his home in Laurel, a suburban community between Baltimore and Washington. After spending time in

Bregman's bedroom, Hassan reportedly went downstairs and unlocked a door. Three armed men wearing masks entered the home, intent on robbery. Bregman was shot multiple times. Lauren Gahn was the FI who went to Bregman's home for the scene investigation.

It didn't take long to catch Hassan and her cohorts. They left plenty of evidence, including security video. All have been charged with first- and second-degree murder.

Not long after Bregman's death, word circulated around the OCME that Fowler's name was among a list of 201 witnesses for the defense of Derek Chauvin, the former Minneapolis police officer charged with the murder of George Floyd.

Fowler was a member of the Forensic Panel, a private organization of expert witnesses. He was the lead of a group of thirteen experts assembled for Chauvin's defense, including six forensic pathologists, a forensic toxicologist, and experts in pharmacology, forensic psychiatry, emergency medicine, and use of force.

Like the rest of America, I watched the video of Chauvin kneeling on Floyd's neck for an agonizing eight minutes and forty-five seconds. Talking with others at work, we couldn't figure out what Fowler could possibly say in Chauvin's defense. At the time, there was no way of knowing how dramatically Fowler's testimony in the Chauvin trial would affect the OCME and me personally.

On the witness stand at Chauvin's trial, Fowler said that Floyd had underlying cardiovascular disease that resulted in a fatal cardiac arrhythmia during his arrest. He also said that Floyd's drug use and exposure to carbon monoxide from the patrol car exhaust contributed to his death, which should be classified as undetermined and not homicide.

The blowback from Fowler's testimony was swift and fierce. I was bombarded with emails and phone calls — vile, vulgar, angry comments. People told me I was corrupt, that I was racist, that I was a tool of a fascist state. I patiently listened to the rants, without arguing or responding in substance, and thanked them for calling.

I'm standing upright and have my clothes on. This is a good day.

Susan Baker emailed to check in on me and offer moral support. That meant a lot.

Dr. Roger Mitchell, former chief medical examiner in Washington, DC, posted a letter online condemning Fowler's testimony and calling for an investigation of in-custody deaths during his tenure. The letter — addressed to Maryland attorney general Brian Frosh, US attorney general Merrick Garland, and Rochelle Walensky, director of the Centers for Disease Control — was signed by more than four hundred individuals, few of whom were forensic pathologists.

Fowler's opinion that the manner of Floyd's death is undetermined "is outside the standard practice and conventions for investigating and certification of in-custody deaths," the letter said. The letter suggested that the OCME of Maryland may be inappropriately using the undetermined and accident manner of death labels to avoid classifying in-custody deaths as homicides and demanded an investigation of all in-custody deaths during the years that Fowler was chief medical examiner, from 2002 until his retirement at the end of 2019.

Mitchell reportedly had a particular interest in the George Floyd investigation. According to court documents filed by attorneys for Tou Thao, the former rookie Minneapolis police officer charged for his role in Floyd's death, Mitchell contacted Dr. Andrew Baker, chief medical examiner of Hennepin County, after his office released a preliminary statement saying that Floyd's autopsy "revealed no physical findings that support a diagnosis of traumatic asphyxia or strangulation." During a phone conversation, Mitchell allegedly told Baker that he would release an editorial critical of his findings. "Mitchell said neck compression has to be in the diagnosis," according to Thao's attorneys. "The final autopsy findings included neck compression."

Three days after Mitchell's letter was posted online, Attorney General Brian Frosh announced that his office would oversee an independent review of in-custody deaths.

When a *Baltimore Sun* reporter called Fowler for his response, he hadn't yet heard about the attorney general's review. He declined to comment specifically on in-custody deaths but defended the OCME's work. "There's a large team of forensic pathologists, with layers of supervision, and those medical examiners always did tremendous work," he said.

The reporter asked Fowler what he thought about a review of in-custody deaths. "People need to do what they need to do," he replied.

By the time a *Washington Post* reporter reached Fowler, he had composed a more thoughtful response. "I stand behind the outstanding work that all of our dedicated staff at the Maryland State Medical Examiner office performed during my tenure as the Chief ME," he said.

The opinion he expressed at the Chauvin trial, Fowler added, was "formulated after the collaboration of thirteen other highly experienced colleagues in multiple disciplines."

There is nothing out of the ordinary about Fowler testifying as an expert witness in a criminal trial. Doctors express opinions in criminal and civil cases every day. Nobody batted an eye when Dr. Jonathan Arden, former chief medical examiner in DC, testified for the defense in the disciplinary hearing of Caesar Goodson, one of the police officers involved in Freddie Gray's death. Arden disputed Allan's conclusion that Freddie Gray's death was a homicide. He said Gray caused his own injury, and his death was an accident. No petitions were circulated.

The idea that the OCME of Maryland doesn't apply homicide

as a manner of death to in-custody fatalities is demonstrably false. Freddie Gray's death was determined to be a homicide, as was that of Anthony Anderson, who sustained broken ribs and a ruptured spleen while being arrested in 2012. And many others.

Not a single in-custody death between 2002 and 2019 was investigated by Fowler. The chief doesn't do autopsies, in part to preserve the public's right to request a change in the cause or manner of death; the chief can't review and reconsider his own work. Each one of those in-custody deaths was the responsibility of staff forensic pathologists. When the chief reviews homicides, as he does with undetermined manner of death and child deaths, he is looking to see that the medical examiner was thorough and complete and that conclusions are supported by facts. But the cause and manner determinations are the medical examiner's call. He doesn't second-guess them.

"That's their opinion, based on the information at hand," he told me. "I'll back them up on it."

In PowerPoint presentations of the OCME's history, Weedn began including a slide with a photo of Fowler testifying at the Derek Chauvin murder trial next to an image of Chauvin kneeling on George Floyd's neck. Many who worked with Fowler felt that this was inflammatory and needlessly disrespectful to him, and by extension to the OCME.

May 6, 2021

I received an email from Michael Pedone, the governor's chief legal counsel. The letter wasn't addressed to the chief medical examiner or the custodian of records. Either one of them would make sense. The letter was addressed to me. "Dear Mr. Goldfarb," the letter began. Oh, this is going to be good.

As you know, Governor Hogan and Attorney General Frosh recently announced efforts to review reports issued by the Office of the Chief Medical Examiner (OCME) regarding in-custody deaths during David Fowler's tenure at OCME. To assist us in beginning this process, please provide me with the preliminary information itemized below as soon as possible, but in any event no later than May 28, 2021.

Pedone defined an in-custody death as one "that occurred while the decedent was deprived of their liberty to any degree by an agent of the government, including during arrest, detention for questioning, or incarceration."

I brought a copy of the letter home to show my wife. It isn't every day that a person is placed in the middle of a national news story. "Michael Pedone? He was my prom date's best friend in high school," she told me.

Of course he was. That's Smalltimore.

Legally, state agencies are represented by the Maryland Office of the Attorney General. Every state entity is assigned an assistant attorney general to serve as legal counsel. The OCME has a lawyer from the AG's office, and the Postmortem Examiners Commission has its own.

To maintain the independence of the external review, I was assigned my own assistant attorney general, a lawyer I could turn to for legal advice. I was fortunate to get James Lewis, who used to represent the OCME until he was rotated to another agency. I knew him, and he knows the OCME. I trusted Lewis to maintain a wall between me, the OCME's counsel, and those within the AG's office conducting the review of in-custody deaths.

I spoke with Lewis a few days after receiving the letter. "There is a reason the letter was addressed to me and not the chief medical examiner or the secretary of health," I said. "Maybe to bypass the chain of authority of the Postmortem Examiners Commission. Whatever the reason, if the governor wanted those people in the loop, the letter would have been addressed to them."

"I believe you're right," Lewis said. "The letter was copied to Dr. Weedn and the attorney general's office. The PDF file itself was named 'Bruce Goldfarb Letter.'"

"As I see it, this is a directive from the state's chief executive to an employee in the executive branch," I said. "This is between the governor's office and me."

"I think your perspective is correct," Lewis said.

This is all on me. Great.

I began by compiling a list of high-profile cases — Freddie Gray, Tyrone West, Anton Black, Anthony Anderson. I checked the website of the American Civil Liberties Union and Facebook pages for Justice for Tyrone West and Black Lives Matter groups, watched YouTube videos of protests to look at the names on signs people held up. The list of names had to be as comprehensive as possible. Any overlooked case invited an accusation of a cover-up.

I spoke with Stephen Janis, who has been covering the issue for years. "I'm putting together the list of in-custody deaths for the attorney general's review," I told him. "If there are any cases that you want to make sure are reviewed, this is your chance. I don't want to miss anything."

Janis never got back to me.

My big problem was how to extract in-custody deaths from the nearly two hundred thousand investigations that were conducted while Fowler was chief. CME, the OCME's computerized database of case records, is searchable by full text. Using "police" as a search term is useless because the police are at the scene of almost every death that comes into the OCME. There would be tens of thousands of results.

I consulted with Spencer-Strong, the OCME's IT programmer. We came up with a list of words that are likely to appear in investigator reports of in-custody deaths: "custody," "arrest," "Taser," "jail," "subdued," "detained," and so on. Running the query produced a list of more than three thousand cases. I spent three days reading through the results. The vast majority of the cases were off-topic, showing up only because an investigator's report said that a decedent's property was in the custody of police or that somebody suffered respiratory arrest.

Reading case after case, I winnowed the list down to three hundred names. I looked the list over. Freddie Gray was on it, but Tyrone West was not. Neither was Robert Ethan Saylor, a man with Down syndrome who died when three off-duty sheriff deputies removed him from a Frederick, Maryland, movie theater in 2013. Or Tyree Woodson, who reportedly shot himself in the bathroom of the Southwest District station while in police custody, supposedly with a handgun stuffed into a boot splint. And several others.

I read investigator reports for these missing cases and developed another list of terms that appeared in those documents: "Mace," "pursuit," "barricade," "excited delirium," and so on. After several iterations, the results included more than thirty thousand cases.

Over a period of more than three weeks, I reviewed investigator reports for these thirty thousand deaths, case after case after case. Each report had to be read thoroughly to determine how police were involved in the death and whether the case fit the criteria defined in Pedone's letter. The list included pedestrians struck during police pursuits, police officers struck by vehicles, cops who took their own lives or killed family members in domestic situations. My days were immersed in narratives of violent confrontations, viciously bloody rampages, and scenes of horrifying mayhem. It was a disturbing experience that haunted my sleep.

The final result was a list of 1,313 deaths. Every name on my list of high-profile cases was included. Not all of these cases were deaths while somebody was being taken into custody. The list included inmates who hanged themselves in Central Processing or overdosed on drugs sneaked into the jail, prisoners who killed each other, people who had a heart attack or stroke while incarcerated, drivers who crashed while being chased by police, instances of "suicide by cop" when somebody deliberately provokes police with a weapon, and people who shot themselves during barricade incidents.

Weedn and others at the OCME suggested ways to compile the list of cases for review. I ignored them. Weedn wanted to make the most of OCME's moment in the spotlight in the cover letter when the list was delivered to the Office of the Attorney General.

"It seems to me that the cover letter is an opportunity to make the case that the OCME needs more resources," he told me.

"No."

"A veiled reference," he said.

"No," I replied. "I'm not going to use the letter to further an agenda or make a point. This letter will likely be released to the public. There will be no whining, no quibbling, and no qualifiers. It's going to be direct and responsive, and nothing else."

"I'd like to have some input on the cover letter," Weedn said.

"No," I told him. "This is going over my signature. This is the assignment I was given. I did the work, and I bear sole responsibility."

"Well, I am your boss," he said.

"So is the governor," I said. "Take it up with him. I have my orders."

Weedn called James Lewis. I listened from the other room as Weedn explained that the review of in-custody deaths reflects on the entire OCME and on him as chief medical examiner, and therefore he should have some involvement. I believe that Lewis told him something to the effect of "stay out of it." Weedn immediately dropped the subject.

A few days later, the chief informed me that Secretary of Health Dennis Schrader and the deputy secretary for public health wanted an update on the review of in-custody deaths. Weedn said that he wanted to be on the call.

Oh hell no. I called Lewis, and he put the kibosh on the meeting. No updates for anybody. This is between me and the governor's office.

I had one last disagreement with the chief during the staff meeting on the morning of May 27, the day that the vetted list of in-custody deaths was to be delivered to the AG's office. Weedn suggested that the list of in-custody deaths should be broken out into categories: police-involved shootings, pursuit-related deaths, fatalities in prisons and jails, and so on.

"I'm not going to do that," I said.

"Why not?" Weedn asked. "It will make things easier for them. They'll want to look at a subset of cases."

"For one thing," I said, "they asked for a list of cases, and that's what I'm going to give them. One list. They didn't ask for lists to be broken out by category. Second, the cases aren't clear-cut. Some pursuits end in shootings. A person can be tased and shot. They can't all be easily categorized. I'm not going to make those judgments. Just one list, as they asked for."

"Well for crying out loud, they're going to come right back and ask for thirteen hundred autopsy reports," Weedn wailed with exasperation. "What do we tell them? This way, we can sort out the cases they're looking for, deaths while people are being taken into custody."

"I have no idea what their next step will be," I said. "Maybe they'll run some statistics, look for differences in manner of death among the medical examiners. Or look for differences between jurisdictions. If I were doing it, I would prioritize the cases that people have been protesting about for years: Tyrone West, Tyree Woodson, Anton Black."

"But we know what cases they're looking for," Weedn said.

I gestured to Mike Eagle, who serves as the OCME's custodian of records, sitting across the table. "We work under a court order that identifies ten fields as public information — the name, date of death, cause and manner, and so on," I said. Eagle nodded. "If you break the list into categories, you're adding information that is not one of those ten fields, and therefore not part of the public record. It can't be released."

Weedn thought for a moment. "Okay, that's a good point," he said.

"We don't know what their next step will be," I said. "Let's wait and see. If they ask for autopsy reports, they'll ask and we'll deal with it."

As I feared, the announcement of the attorney general's review of in-custody deaths unleashed a flurry of inquiries. Several people called and asked for Fowler's contact information, which I declined to provide. They expressed candid opinions of Fowler's testimony in the Chauvin trial and suggested forms of violence to inflict on him. Others informed me that I was employed by a racist organization complicit in covering up police misconduct. I chose not to engage in a discussion and thanked them for calling.

Several people called to demand that certain cases be reviewed. The mother of a man who hung himself in Central Processing insisted that his investigation be reopened. She claimed that her son was murdered, although he was alone in a cell and the exterior corridor outside his door was under continuous security video. Nobody else went in or out of his cell until he was discovered slumped with a bedsheet tied around his neck. His mother had already gone through the appeals process. The investigation was reviewed by Fowler and the secretary of health, who referred the matter to an administrative judge. The manner of death remained suicide. Nonetheless, I assured the woman that her son's name was on the list of in-custody deaths provided to the attorney general. Whether they review the case is up to them.

I received several letters from prisoners claiming that the investigations into the deaths of which they are accused were inherently biased because they occurred on Fowler's watch.

"Over 400 medical professionals recently wrote to state officials questioning Fowler's credibility and alleging that the office during his tenure often sided with the police and prosecutors," one resident at the Eastern Correctional Institution wrote. Much of the rest of his letter was about the testimony of the medical examiner who investigated his victim.

Out of curiosity, I looked online to see what this prisoner had done. According to news accounts, he beat and kicked his girlfriend, who was twenty-seven weeks pregnant with his baby, for a period of twelve hours. Her jaw was broken, her lip split, a gash opened over her swollen right eye, bruises on her arms and legs. The medical examiner testified that the fetus was normal for its gestational age and was otherwise viable until the placenta tore away from the uterine wall due to the assault. My correspondent was convicted of manslaughter of the fetus and first-degree assault and sentenced to thirty-five years in prison.

I seethed while composing a terse reply.

> I am responding to your May 3 letter regarding the death for which you were convicted. The review of which you speak is related to in-custody deaths, not other cases investigated by the Office of the Chief Medical Examiner. In any event, the review is being conducted by the Attorney General's office, and not this agency. I suggest you direct any comments to them.

Good luck, you sick bastard.

Morale around the OCME staff was low. People were openly grumbling, talking about looking for work elsewhere. Autopsy cases continued to pour in with no respite in sight. One morning's conference sheet had twenty-eight cases for autopsies. Only two medical examiners and two autopsy techs were available, with others out sick or testifying in court. All twenty-eight cases were done by the two teams.

As predicted, mistakes happened. Shortcuts were taken to keep up with the pace. Evidence was misplaced. An autopsy technician handling two cases at once — a violation of policies and procedures — erroneously switched identity bracelets on the bodies.

"I came to this state to work here," Kristine Tricario, a forensic investigator, said to me. "This was the pinnacle, a beacon. The OCME is so admired, has such a reputation for excellence. I want to live up to that. But I don't know what's happening. It's like a free fall. We need to get back to what it used to be."

Whenever a body is found in the Inner Harbor, rumors of a serial killer buzz over social media. People say that a malevolent figure lurks the waterfront at night, pushing unsuspecting victims into the murky water. That's an exciting story, and easy to believe if a person only pays attention to drownings within an arbitrarily defined geographic boundary.

The truth is more mundane. Scores of people drown in Maryland every year, sixty to seventy people. Few of these deaths make the news.

Maryland is a very watery state. About 22 percent of the state's surface area is water, mainly Chesapeake Bay, the nation's largest estuary. Between the Atlantic coast, the bay, and associated waterways, Maryland has more than seventy-seven hundred miles of coastline. The City of Baltimore itself has more than sixty miles of shoreline, including popular areas of the Inner

Harbor, Fells Point, and Canton lined with restaurants and bars. Along much of the waterfront, there are no barriers to keep people from stumbling into the water.

Once a person falls into the harbor, there is little chance of getting out alive. Most of the harbor is lined with a steel piling bulkhead several feet above the waterline, sheer wall with no grips or ladders. Areas of the Inner Harbor are on piers, with water extending beneath the streets. A person can easily get disoriented and trapped. The water is so dangerous that first responders won't jump in to rescue a drowning victim.

People drown in Chesapeake Bay and the Atlantic beach off Ocean City with regularity. They drown in ponds and backyard pools, in raging flash floods, in bathtubs and in shallow creeks. I read a report about a forty-seven-year-old man out boating and drinking with friends. He dove into the water to retrieve his hat and didn't resurface. A person can slip away that easily.

After work hours one August evening, Charlie Gischlar, public information officer for the Department of Health and a former WBAL radio newsman, sent me an email with a link to a story about a seventeen-year-old young man whose body was found off the Ocean City beach. Gischlar fielded media inquiries across the entire department, which sometimes included the medical examiner office. We were in touch often, particularly when a death involved a celebrity or was otherwise newsworthy.

This email was unusual in an understated way. "We will likely get cause and manner requests on this," was all he said. Gischlar usually reached out after being contacted by a reporter. It wasn't like him to get ahead of something routine and ordinary like this. I wondered if this was something personal for him, whether he knew the victim's family, but I didn't want to probe.

I told Gischlar that the seventeen-year-old would be on the next day's conference sheet and that I'd let him know as soon as I heard something. "Roger that. Tragic," he wrote. "My kid loves swimming in OC and is near that age. Hits home."

"Every day here I am reminded of a relative or friend," I replied. "Hug your kids."

The investigator's report was heartbreaking to read. The kid was from Pennsylvania, visiting Ocean City with a group of friends. He was not a skilled swimmer and remained in water no deeper than his waist. A couple of his buddies were within yards of him when a rip current swiftly dragged him out into deeper water, and then he was gone. Just like that. The report noted that the kid's mother, back home in Pennsylvania, was so distraught it was impossible to get information on his social and medical history.

I told Gischlar that the kid was apparently caught in a rip current.

"Such a tragedy," he said. "My daughter loves the ocean. When she was little, we got caught in a weak rip. I knew what to do. First, relax, do not panic. Second, let it take you until it eases, then swim perpendicular to escape."

What a terrifying fate, helplessly swept away by forces beyond control.

EPILOGUE

The mood at the OCME was sullen as the staff grew increasingly restive. Ten months into Weedn's tenure, and nothing had been done to ease the workload. No new assistant medical examiners were recruited, and the cases continued to climb.

On December 10, 2021, Weedn instituted a daily limit on autopsies. No more than three autopsies per medical examiner each day. Depending on how many doctors were on the schedule, cases were limited to twelve to fifteen per day. Any decedents who were received once the limit was reached were held over and put on the next day's conference sheet. With an average of twenty-three bodies received by the OCME every day, a backlog began to accumulate quickly.

In ten days there was a backlog of more than fifty cases waiting for autopsy. By January 13 there were more than a hundred decedents on the schedule for autopsy, exceeding the capacity of the OCME's two walk-in body refrigerators. Gurneys with body bags lined the unrefrigerated corridors of the autopsy suite.

Thursday morning's staff meeting was contentious. It was clear that Weedn had no game plan, no exit strategy, no notions about how to dig the OCME out of a hole getting deeper by the day.

"This isn't going to work," Tom Brown said. "Let's just lock the door and leave."

"What am I supposed to do?" Weedn asked.

"Plan for two hundred bodies," I said.

A week later there were 150 bodies waiting for autopsy, and by February 1 the backlog exceeded 200 cases. Decedents were held for two weeks or more until they could be examined. Families were unable to bury their kin according to religious custom, by the next sunset by the strictures of Orthodox Judaism and within twenty-four hours by the tenets of Islam. Many bodies were too decomposed for an open casket viewing. Criminal investigations were delayed, including homicides and a possible case of infant neglect.

Complaints were inevitable. Weedn directed that all complaints be directed to me. For weeks I was inundated with irate phone calls and emails. People contacted elected officials, state lawmakers, and the governor's office. One woman emailed me photos of her daughter's decomposed body. "Look at her," she demanded of me. "This is how I had to say good-bye to my baby girl."

People pleaded for help. The son of a man who died suddenly was on bereavement leave from his deployment in Iraq. His mother called to see whether the body could be released to a funeral home so their son could be present at his father's funeral. I was told to give no specific dates for an autopsy; it could be a week or longer. The kid was shipped back to Iraq, unable to attend his father's funeral.

Families scheduled funerals. Death announcements were published. People had already traveled for a funeral that couldn't be held because the body wasn't released from the medical examiner office. I heard from people who traveled from Australia, Europe, and across the United States. They'd already spent money on airfare and hotels, taking leave from work, and couldn't return in a week or two.

All I could do was apologize. There are no words to make it right.

The Department of Health activated a temporary morgue, known as Metro West, that was set up for Covid in the parking garage of an unused office building that formerly housed the Social Security Administration. Decedents who had been examined and were ready for release to a funeral home were transferred to Metro West to make room in the OCME's body refrigerators. Three 20-foot refrigerated trailers were installed in the first-floor garage, each holding seven bodies (twenty-one with shelving installed), increased the OCME's capacity.

Still, the limit on autopsies meant that the backlog increased unabated, reaching a peak of 240 bodies lined up for examination.

The OCME made the news, in a bad way that Ripple and others had warned about. Jayne Miller, investigative reporter for WBAL News, broke the story on January 18, 2022. Other local news outlets picked up the story, including *Maryland Matters* and *Baltimore Banner*, and major media *The Baltimore Sun* and *Washington Post*. Reporters told stories of families outraged about decomposed bodies and delayed funerals, which were picked up by wire services and national publications from blogs to *Huffington Post* and *USA Today*.

Whatever goodwill the OCME had banked was depleted. The public image of the agency now is of incompetence and callous indifference.

Mike Eagle announced his resignation in mid-February. Along with Brian Tannenbaum, two-thirds of the OCME's IT department was now gone. Aside from heading up IT, Eagle was also custodian of records and integral to the smooth operation of the agency.

During 2021 the OCME conducted about eighteen thousand investigations — an 80 percent increase in a decade. During the same time period, the agency's budget kept up with inflation but made no accommodations for workload. When I began work at the OCME, the agency had eighty-four full-time employees. At last count there are sixty-three.

With Eagle's departure, only a handful of experienced senior staff remained. Tom Brown joined the OCME about six months before I did. The OCME was at risk of losing the continuity of institutional memory — who did what, where things are kept, how things are done.

On the morning of February 18, the Postmortem Examiners Commission held a closed-door session to discuss the OCME crisis. By noon, Weedn announced his resignation.

The State of Maryland threw in the towel and asked the Federal Emergency Management Agency for help. FEMA sent in a team of volunteer forensic pathologists and technicians from the Disaster Mortuary Operational Response Team (DMORT), the organization that assists after large-scale natural disasters such as Hurricane Katrina in 2005 and the 2010 Haiti earthquake.

Once an exemplar of forensic medicine excellence, a gold standard for the field, the OCME turned into a man-made disaster.

The OCME's medical examiners, with the help of DMORT volunteers, reduced the autopsy backlog within three weeks. Since then, the agency has remained free of a backlog. But its situation is tenuous.

Whether the OCME can pull out of its years-long tailspin is still questionable. The opioid epidemic shows no signs of abating. New, more powerful synthetic opioids continue to emerge on the streets. The crisis in which the OCME finds itself is not unique to Maryland.

The scarcity of forensic pathologists and adequate funding remains a chronic problem nationwide. Forensic pathologists simply aren't being produced in a quantity to replace medical examiners who retire or leave the profession. At present, there are only five hundred to seven hundred forensic pathologists practicing in the United States. A recent report to Congress from the National Institute of Justice estimates that eleven hundred to twelve hundred forensic pathologists are needed right now to perform forensic autopsies. And yet interest in pursuing forensic pathology as a career is declining. Of eighteen thousand doctors graduating from US medical schools every year, only about three hundred (1.7 percent) choose a residency in pathology. Approximately 13 percent of these pathology residents will continue to a fellowship in forensic pathology, and of these individuals, perhaps two-thirds, or only thirty-seven of them, will become board-certified forensic pathologists and join the workforce each year.

To handle the forensic investigation needs of Maryland's population of six million people and stay within the 250-case annual limit for National Association of Medical Examiners accreditation, the OCME should have a roster of twenty-six medical examiners. By the middle of 2022, the agency is expected to have only seven forensic pathologists on staff. The average caseload per medical examiner is projected to exceed seven hundred in 2022 and more than fifteen hundred in the following year. Obviously, that won't happen. No competent forensic pathologist can perform five hundred, six hundred, or more autopsies in a year.

Even with its deficiencies, the quality of forensic investigation in Maryland is still better than what is provided in most of the United States. About half of the US population is under the jurisdiction of coroners and lacks access to qualified forensic pathologists in well-equipped medical examiner offices. If a crisis can occur in a progressive and well-managed system such as Maryland, the quality of death investigation in less-developed parts of the country are left to the imagination.

In states including Wisconsin, Missouri, Indiana, Illinois, New York, Idaho, Georgia, Colorado, and Nevada, elected coroners aren't required to have any medical or legal training before they certify the cause and manner of death. In Missouri, for example, the requirements to serve as a county coroner are that a person is over the age of twenty-one, has lived in the state for at least a year, and has resided in the county in which he or she intends to serve for at least six months. And, of course, gets more votes than anybody else. By comparison, the requirements for a barber's license in Missouri include completing fifteen hundred hours of training and passing a test. To be a nail technician and legally give a manicure in Missouri, a person must complete four hundred hours of training and pass a test. But if a person is elected coroner, they can crack open a beer and start signing death certificates.

Many medical examiners lack essential facilities — one-third don't have an in-house toxicology laboratory, and an equal number are without X-ray equipment — much less the resources to adopt processes and systems to address chronic problems such as preventing theft and tracking bodies. Scandals and crises have plagued coroner and medical examiner offices in New York City, San Francisco, Las Vegas, Detroit, Ohio, Colorado, and elsewhere.

Autopsy backlogs have been reported recently in West Virginia, Alameda County, Atlanta, New Hampshire, Boston, and many other medical examiner offices throughout the country. In Mississippi, which has only two forensic pathologists covering the entire state, the backlog of autopsy reports was so bad that it often took years — up to five years — for the written report to be completed, delaying the filing of criminal charges and prosecutions.

The Boston medical examiner office addressed the backlog problem by performing fewer autopsies. In recent years, the office has reduced the number of autopsies from 44 percent of cases to 26–27 percent, far below the national average of 38 percent in statewide offices, according to a National Institute of Justice study. Only Maine and New Mexico have lower autopsy rates, according to a *Boston Globe* report, at 10 percent and 21 percent, respectively. Rather than the traditional autopsy, an increasing number of cases are investigated by reviewing medical records and looking at photographs. These "chart review" cases increased fourfold in three years. Are some homicides missed by less-than-thorough examination? Maybe.

"We've all seen cases that come in and look like a straightforward drug overdose. And then you do an autopsy and find out this person was strangled," Dr. James Gill, chief medical examiner in Connecticut, told a *Boston Globe* reporter. "That's the nightmare scenario. That's what you don't want to miss."

Problems in forensic medicine are not limited to the United States. Backlogs in forensic autopsies have been reported from Canada, the United Kingdom, New Zealand, and many places around the world.

The crisis in forensic death investigation has profound implications for every American. The next death needing a competent, qualified forensic investigation could be any one of us.

NOTES

Chapter 1: Once in a Lifetime

1 **Hunched over by the front door . . .**
Baltimore BLOC, "Day 414, West Wednesday, Medical Examiner's Office," YouTube, https://youtu.be/XbdI-t_O1fk. Accessed March 19, 2022.

2 **A few years ago, he was charged . . .**
Robert Lang, "Not Guilty Verdict for Man Who Left Toilet at Courthouse," WBAL, September 15, 2011, https://www.wbal.com/article/80020/3/not-guilty-verdict-for-man-who-left-toilet-at-courthouse. Accessed March 19, 2022.

3 **The complete autopsy report was published . . .**
"Officers in Tyrone West Death Will Not Be Charged," *Baltimore Sun*, December 19, 2013, https://www.baltimoresun.com/maryland/baltimore-city/bs-md-ci-tyrone-west-20131219-story.html. Accessed March 19, 2022.

4 **That's a violation of COMAR . . .**
Sec. 10.35.01.14, Release of Medical Examiner's Records, Code of Maryland Regulations, http://mdrules.elaws.us/comar/10.35.01.14. Accessed March 19, 2022.

4 **On the day 223 West Wednesday . . .**
Baltimore BLOC, "Day 223, West Wednesday, Family of Tyrone West at the Medical Examiner's Office," YouTube, February 27, 2014, https://www.youtube.com/watch?v=5QHOolH7mEA. Accessed March 19, 2022.

10 The unemployment rate in the OCME's neighborhood . . .

"The Right Investment? Corrections Spending in Baltimore City," Justice Policy Institute, February 2015, https://justicepolicy.org/research/the-right-investment-corrections-spending-in-baltimore-city. Accessed March 19, 2022.

2013–2017 American Community Survey 5-Year Estimates, US Census Bureau, 2018, https://www.census.gov/programs-surveys/acs/data.html. Accessed March 19, 2022.

Criminal Victimization, 2018, Bureau of Justice Statistics, https://www.bjs.gov/index.cfm?ty=tp&tid=31. Accessed March 19, 2022.

Baltimore City 2017 Neighborhood Health Profile, Baltimore City Health Department, June 2017, https://health.baltimorecity.gov/neighborhoods/neighborhood-health-profile-reports. Accessed March 19, 2022.

13 At a holiday party at my nursing instructor's home . . .

Jon Franklin and Alan Doelp, *Shock-Trauma* (New York: St. Martin's Press, 1980).

Chapter 2: The Dead House

Portions of this chapter are adapted from "Death Investigation in Maryland," by Bruce Goldfarb, in *The History of the National Association of Medical Examiners* (2016), 235–64, https://www.thename.org/assets/docs/NAME%20e-book%202016%20final%2006-14-16.pdf. Accessed March 19, 2022.

21 ". . . mephitic fly-by-night schools . . ."

H. L. Mencken, "University of Maryland School of Medicine," *Baltimore Evening Sun*, May 28, 1937.

22 ". . . a dead house, in which to deposit dead bodies"

Annual Session of the City Council, *Baltimore Sun*, February 2, 1861, 4.

22 The following year, Dr. Charles H. Bradford . . .

Ordinances of the Mayor and City Council of Baltimore (Baltimore: King Bros. & Armiger, 1862), 440–41.

24 Noting that there were five dissecting rooms . . .

J. S. Lynch, A. Friedenwald, C. F. Bevan, and T. Ople, "The Morgue Question," *Baltimore Sun*, June 5, 1885, 1.

24 "In the name of the afflicted friends of the unknown dead . . ."

Annual Report of the Health Department of the City of Baltimore, 1888 (Baltimore: John Cox, 1889), 13.

25 "The building now used as a morgue . . ."
"Need of a New Morgue: Coroner Tells Commissioners That It Is
Urgent," *Baltimore Sun*, October 12, 1900, 12.

26 "Aside from the nasty, dirty and partly dangerous . . ."
"Says the Morgue Is in Horrible Condition," *Baltimore Sun*, March 29,
1919, 6.

27 ". . . the stench cannot be overcome . . ."
"Says New Morgue Is Needed at Once," *Baltimore Sun*, February 7, 1924,
3.

28 "We should build the morgue with a view to future needs"
"To Complete New Morgue by Oct. 1925," *Baltimore Sun*, February 1,
1924, 9.

29 "It's a known fact . . ."
Howard J. Maldeis, "Medical Examiner's System in the State of
Maryland," *Southern Medical Journal* 41, no. 9 (1943): 840–44.

31 "One of the most important duties . . ."
Maldeis, "Medical Examiner's System in the State of Maryland."

31 Lee praised a young pathologist . . .
Letter from Frances Glessner Lee to Francis I. McGarraghy and others,
June 5, 1951, Glessner House museum, Chicago.

32 Grammer, a thirty-three-year-old Sunday school teacher . . .
Nathan Miller, "Some Dead Men Do Tell Tales," *Baltimore Sun*, May 28,
1959, 20.
Randi Henderson, "Maryland's Main Man at the Morgue," *Baltimore Sun*,
September 12, 1982, E1.

33 "Dr. Fisher has trained more people . . ."
Charles S. Petty, "Russell S. Fisher, MD, Physician, Pathologist, Teacher
(1916–1984)," *American Journal of Clinical Pathology* 84, no. 2 (August 1,
1985): 254–55.

34 "Dr. Fisher was very broad-minded . . ."
Personal interview with Virginia Ryker, 2015–2017.

34 "Less than the money it takes . . ."
"Fisher Tells 'How Doctor Plays Detective,'" *Baltimore Sun*, October 1,
1955, 4.

34 "No matter where you go throughout the United States . . ."
Erle Staley Gardner, *The Case of the Moth-Eaten Mink* (New York:
William Morrow, 1952).

35 **"I was taken to a very dilapidated part of town . . ."**
"A Posthumous Award and Tribute to the Late Russell S. Fisher," Werner
Spitz presentation at American Academy of Forensic Sciences,
February 18, 1988, *OCME News*, May 1988, 3–4.

36 **"Smialek had his own way of doing things . . ."**
Personal interview with Virginia Ryker, 2015–2017.

Chapter 3: Beginnings

38 **The other two papers on my desk . . .**
Postmortem Examiners Commission, Annotated Code of Maryland
Health — General, Title 5, Subtitle 3, Westlaw, Maryland Law and
Court Rules, https://govt.westlaw.com/mdc/Index. Accessed April 5,
2022.
Postmortem Examiners Commission, Title 10, Subtitle 35, COMAR
Online, State of Maryland, Division of State Documents, http://www
.dsd.state.md.us/COMAR/ComarHome.html. Accessed April 4, 2022.

40 **The OCME is subject to a court order . . .**
Public Information Act, General Provisions, Title 4, Maryland Law and
Court Rules.

44 **"Buffing and turfing . . ."**
Samuel Shem, *The House of God* (New York: Richard Marek Publishers,
1978).

45 **"The health and welfare of this organization . . ."**
Personal interview with Virginia Ryker, 2015–2017.

54 **Thursday, July 18, 2013, was a hot day . . .**
This section is based on the report of the Independent Review Board,
"In-Custody Fatality Independent Review Board for the Death of
Tyrone West: Findings and Recommendations," August 8, 2014,
https://www.scribd.com/document/236257430/Baltimore-Police
-independent-report-into-Tyrone-West-death. Accessed March 20,
2022.
Justin Fenton, "Tyrone West Files Show Passenger's Account of Death
in Police Custody," *Baltimore Sun*, January 23, 2014, https://www
.baltimoresun.com/news/crime/bs-md-ci-tyrone-west-witness
-20140122-story.html. Accessed March 20, 2022.

58 **Manner of death is a categorization . . .**
National Association of Medical Examiners, A Guide for Manner of
Death Classification, https://name.memberclicks.net/assets/docs/
MANNEROFDEATH.pdf. Accessed April 5, 2022.

Chapter 4: Smalltimore

63 My story for *Patch* . . .
Bruce Goldfarb, "Details Emerge in Brutal Lansdowne Slaying," *Arbutus Patch*, October 26, 2011, https://patch.com/maryland/arbutus/details-of-brutal-lansdowne-slaying-emerge. Accessed March 20, 2022.

68 "A health officer may take control of a body . . ."
Annotated Code of Maryland Health — General, Title 5, Subtitle 506, Westlaw, Maryland Law and Court Rules, https://govt.westlaw.com/mdc/Index. Accessed April 5, 2022.

68 In the late 1990s, an Arundel County man . . .
"Father Says He Panicked, Buried 3-Year-Old," *Washington Post*, August 25, 1999, https://www.washingtonpost.com/archive/local/1999/08/25/father-says-he-panicked-buried-3-year-old/9687e21e-f879-4932-a9a0-8fbec48ab2c0/. Accessed March 20, 2022.

69 The podcast episode featured stories . . .
"Justice Talking," Stoop Storytelling series, March 18, 2013, https://stoopstorytelling.com/event/justice-talking/. Accessed March 20, 2022.

70 "The Nose," an un-bylined media critic column . . .
"Habeus Crapus: Baltimore Examiner Blows Stories About Serial Killer Out of Proportion," *Baltimore City Paper*, November 8, 2006.

72 Bodies get dumped in Baltimore . . .
"The Bodies of Leakin Park," http://chamspage.blogspot.com/2010/11/the-bodies-of-leakin-park-baltimore-md.html. Accessed March 20, 2022.

75 The accreditation process involves a site visit . . .
National Association of Medical Examiners, Inspection and Accreditation, https://www.thename.org/inspection-accreditation. Accessed April 5, 2022.
National Association of Medical Examiners, NAME Accreditation Checklist, https://www.thename.org/assets/docs/NAME%20Accreditation%20Checklist%202019%20-%202024.pdf. Accessed April 5, 2022.

81 Before my time at the OCME, Fowler had made one exception . . .
FilmRise True Crime, *Forensic Files*, Season 6, episode 12, "Whodunit," YouTube, August 6, 2001, https://youtu.be/a1TKzRLAW28. Accessed April 5, 2022.

83 **Following considerable negotiation of the ground rules . . .**
"Hidden Maryland: Office of the Chief Medical Examiner," *Baltimore Sun*, July 29, 2013, http://darkroom.baltimoresun.com/2013/07/hidden-maryland-office-of-the-chief-medical-examiner/#1. Accessed March 20, 2022.

83 **In October 2014, I began listening to the *Serial* podcast . . .**
Serial podcast, https://serialpodcast.org/season-one. Accessed April 5, 2022.

Chapter 5: The Next One

85 **"I'm all about trying to get government off our backs . . ."**
John Wagner and Arelis Hernandez, "Candidates for Governor of Maryland Make Late Appeals," *Washington Post*, November 2, 2014, https://www.washingtonpost.com/local/md-politics/candidates-for-governor-of-maryland-make-late-appeals/2014/11/02/402485da-62bb-11e4-bb14-4cfea1e742d5_story.html. Accessed March 19, 2022.

87 **Medical examiners in New Mexico . . .**
Charles J. Van Hook, "Hantavirus Pulmonary Syndrome — The 25th Anniversary of the Four Corners Outbreak," *Emerging Infectious Diseases* 24, no. 11 (November 2018): 2056–060, https://www.ncbi.nlm.nih.gov/pmc/articles/PMC6199996/. Accessed March 14, 2022.
"CDC Grand Rounds: Discovering New Diseases via Enhanced Partnership Between Public Health and Pathology Experts," *Morbidity and Mortality Weekly Report* (February 14, 2014): 121–26, https://www.cdc.gov/mmwr/preview/mmwrhtml/mm6306a1.htm. Accessed March 14, 2022.

87 **Based on an unusual cluster of four pediatric deaths . . .**
Lydia Aguilera, "Pediatric OTC Cough and Cold Product Safety," *US Pharmacist*, July 20, 2009, https://www.uspharmacist.com/article/pediatric-otc-cough-and-cold-product-safety. Accessed March 14, 2022.
"Babies' Cold Drugs Pulled from Shelves: What's a Parent to Do?" *Seattle Times*, October 12, 2007, https://www.seattletimes.com/nation-world/babies-cold-drugs-pulled-from-shelves-whats-a-parent-to-do/. Accessed March 14, 2022.

87 **At one point, the Los Angeles coroner . . .**
Elaine Woo, "LA County Coroner Had Low-Key Style," *Los Angeles Times*, September 27, 2008, https://www.latimes.com/archives/la-xpm-2008-sep-27-me-kornblum27-story.html. Accessed March 14, 2022.

88 Katie Mingle, a producer for the *99% Invisible* podcast . . .
99% Invisible, episode 165, "The Nutshell Studies," May 19, 2015,
https://99percentinvisible.org/episode/the-nutshell-studies/.
Accessed March 19, 2022.

98 Allan's examination revealed that Gray . . .
Will Greenberg, "Leaked Autopsy Report Finds Freddie Gray Suffered
'High-Energy' Injury," *Washington Post*, June 24, 2015, https://www
.washingtonpost.com/news/morning-mix/wp/2015/06/24/leaked
-autopsy-finds-freddie-gray-suffered-high-energy-injury/. Accessed
April 5, 2022.

99 That morning, a story by Stephen Janis . . .
"Freddie Gray Supporters Wary of Medical Examiner," Real News
Network, May 1, 2015, https://therealnews.com/sjaniso501meturstf.
Accessed March 19, 2022.

102 My well-worn copy . . .
Susan P. Baker, Brian O'Neill, and Ronald S. Karpf, *Injury Fact Book*
(Lexington, MA: Lexington Books, 1984).

Chapter 6: An Abundance of Caution

109 Although well intended, there is no evidence . . .
"Position Statement Opposed to Autopsy Observation as a Form of
Punishment," National Association of Medical Examiners, March 9,
2001, https://name.memberclicks.net/assets/docs/a23eed51-73f5-4c11
-b4eb-ba457112572c.pdf. Accessed April 11, 2022.

113 On the morning conference sheet . . .
"Man Dies Following Baltimore Building Collapse," WBAL-TV News,
March 29, 2016, https://www.wbaltv.com/article/man-dies-following
-baltimore-building-collapse/7099749. Accessed April 11, 2022.
Christian Schaffer, "Police ID Man Killed in Building Collapse on Car,"
WMAR-TV News, March 29, 2016, https://www.wmar2news.com/
news/region/baltimore-city/police-identify-man-who-died-after
-building-collapsed-on-his-car. Accessed April 11, 2022.
Tim Prudente, "When Vacant House Fell in West Baltimore, a Retiree
Was Crushed in His Prized Cadillac," *Baltimore Sun*, March 20, 2016,
https://www.baltimoresun.com/maryland/baltimore-city/bs-md-ci
-cadillac-crushed-20160329-story.html. Accessed April 11, 2022.

123 In the predawn darkness of November 1, 2016 . . .
"School Bus Collision with a Transit Bus," National Transportation Safety

Board, Accident HWY17MH007, https://www.ntsb.gov/
investigations/Pages/HWY17MH007.aspx. Accessed April 11, 2022.
Lynh Bui and Dana Hedgpeth, "Six Killed in Baltimore After School Bus
and Commuter Bus Collide," *Washington Post*, November 1, 2016,
https://www.washingtonpost.com/local/public-safety/six-killed-in
-baltimore-after-school-bus-and-commuter-bus-collide/2016/11/01/
fda84d4a-a043-11e6-8d63-3e0a660f1f04_story.html. Accessed April 11,
2022.
"Frederick Avenue Bus Crash Leaves Six Dead," *Baltimore Brew*,
November 1, 2016, https://www.baltimorebrew.com/2016/11/01/
frederick-avenue-bus-crash-leaves-six-dead/. Accessed April 11, 2022.
Scott Dance and Colin Campbell, "Driver in Fatal Crash Had History of
Crashes, Seizures, NTSB Report Says," *Baltimore Sun*, December 7,
2016, https://www.baltimoresun.com/maryland/baltimore-city/bs-md
-bus-crash-ntsb-report-20161207-story.html. Accessed April 11, 2016.

Chapter 7: Cops and Robbers

131 **The Baltimore Police Department, still bruised by the aftermath . . .**
Although not relied upon for this book, recent works about the Gun
Trace Task Force include *We Own This City* by Justin Fenton (New
York: Random House, 2021) and *I Got a Monster* by Baynard Woods and
Brandon Soderberg (New York: St. Martin's Press, 2020).

131 **". . . 1930s-style gangsters . . ."**
"Indicted Baltimore Officers Were Like '1930s-Style Gangsters,'" BBC
News, March 2, 2017, https://www.bbc.com/news/world-us-canada
-39145361. Accessed April 11, 2022.

131 **A month after the GTTF officers' arrest . . .**
"Investigation of the Baltimore City Police Department," US Department
of Justice, Civil Rights Division, August 10, 2016, https://www.justice
.gov/crt/file/883296/download. Accessed November 8, 2021.
Consent Decree Monitoring Team for Baltimore City, https://www
.bpdmonitor.com/. Accessed November 8, 2021.
Consent Decree Basics, Baltimore City Police Department, https://www
.baltimorepolice.org/transparency/consent-decree-basics. Accessed
November 8, 2021.

142 **Rahim, forty-one years old, was a quiet guy . . .**
Justin Fenton, "Cousin of Baltimore Gun Trace Task Force Detective
Gets 5 Years in Prison for Helping with Robbery," *Baltimore Sun*, March
9, 2018, https://www.baltimoresun.com/news/crime/bs-md-ci-rahim
-gttf-sentencing-20180309-story.html. Accessed April 11, 2022.

"Second Man Pleads Guilty to Robbery with Member of the Baltimore
Police Gun Trace Task Force," US Department of Justice, US Attorney's
Office, District of Maryland, https://www.justice.gov/usao-md/pr/
second-man-pleads-guilty-robbery-member-baltimore-police-gun
-trace-task-force. Accessed April 11, 2022.

148 On the afternoon of Wednesday, November 15, 2017 . . .
"Report to the Commissioner of the Police Department of Baltimore
City Concerning an Independent Review of the November 15, 2017
Incident and Its Aftermath," August 27, 2018, https://www.
baltimorepolice.org/sites/default/files/General%20Website%20PDFs/
Suiter%20Report%20Public.pdf. Accessed April 11, 2022.
Justin Fenton, "FBI Confronted Baltimore Det. Suiter Weeks Before His
Death with Allegation That He Planted Drugs, Memo Says," *Baltimore
Sun*, January 28, 2021, https://www.baltimoresun.com/news/crime/
bs-pr-md-ci-cr-gttf-suiter-new-fbi-document-20210128-
ieeuixonondbzchvbpf2yg3sye-story.html. Accessed April 11, 2022.
Nick Schager, "Sean Suiter Was About to Testify Against His Fellow
Cops. Then He Wound Up Dead," *Daily Beast*, December 7, 2021,
https://www.thedailybeast.com/sean-suiter-was-about-to-testify
-against-his-fellow-baltimore-cops-then-he-wound-up-dead. Accessed
April 11, 2022.

Chapter 8: Tipping Point

160 As I was talking with the family . . .
"Baltimore County Officer Amy Caprio Killed; Suspects in Custody,"
CBS Baltimore, May 21, 2018, https://baltimore.cbslocal.com/2018
/05/21/baltimore-county-officer-shot/. Accessed April 12, 2022.
Matthew Haag, "4 Teenagers Charged in Killing of Baltimore County
Officer with Jeep," *New York Times*, May 22, 2018, https://www.ny
times.com/2018/05/22/us/baltimore-police-officer-shot-killed.html.
Accessed April 12, 2022.
Justin Jouvenal, Peter Hermann, and Dana Hedgpeth, "16-Year-Old
Charged with Running Over and Killing Maryland Police Officer Faced
Court Monitoring for Previous Cases," *Washington Post*, May 22, 2018,
https://www.washingtonpost.com/local/public-safety/16-year-old
-arrested-in-maryland-police-officers-death-three-others-sought/2018
/05/22/5c67d840-5db8-11e8-b2b8-08a538d9dbd6_story.html. Accessed
April 12, 2022.

161 Jarrod Ramos held a grudge against the *Capital Gazette* . . .
"Capital Gazette Shooting," *Capital Gazette*, https://www.capitalgazette.

com/topic/capital-gazette-shooting-topic.html. Accessed April 12, 2022.

Capital Gazette Staff, "What to Know About the Capital Gazette Shooting Case," *Capital Gazette*, June 23, 2021, https://www.capitalgazette.com/news/crime/ac-cn-capital-gazette-trial-updates-20191028-kuhqsr55b5al7aenqwangehbsa-story.html. Accessed April 12, 2022.

Katie Mettler and Emily Davies, "Capital Gazette Gunman Sentenced to Life in Prison Without Parole for Rampage That Killed 5," *Washington Post*, September 28, 2021, https://www.washingtonpost.com/local/public-safety/jarrod-ramos-sentence-capital-gazette-shooting/2021/09/27/50aad956-1d6f-11ec-bcb8-0cb135811007_story.html. Accessed April 12, 2022.

163 "I'm a police reporter . . ."

Ryan W. Miller, "Capital Gazette Shooting: Reporter Describes Scene 'Like a War Zone' in Annapolis Newsroom," *USA Today*, June 28, 2018. https://www.usatoday.com/story/news/nation/2018/06/28/capital-gazette-shooting-reporter-phil-davis-calls-scene-warzone/743737002/. Accessed April 12, 2022.

163 In the spring of 2018 . . .

"Report to the Commissioner of the Police Department of Baltimore City Concerning an Independent Review of the November 15, 2017 Incident and Its Aftermath." Independent Review Board, August 27, 2018. https://www.baltimorepolice.org/sites/default/files/General%20Website%20PDFs/Suiter%20Report%20Public.pdf. Accessed October 8, 2022.

167 In October 2020, the City of Baltimore . . .

Ryan Dickstein, Kelly Broderick, and Amira Hairston, "Board Approves $900K in Worker's Comp to Family of Former BPD Detective Sean Suiter," WMAR-2 News, October 23, 2020, https://www.wmar2news.com/news/local-news/city-to-pay-workers-compensation-to-family-of-detective-sean-suiter. Accessed April 12, 2022.

Chapter 9: Going to Ground

173 One of the tours I conducted through the OCME . . .

Chesapeake Search Dogs, https://chesapeakesearchdogs.org/. Accessed April 12, 2022.

177 Sam had grown so alarmed . . .

Bad Batch Alert, http://www.badbatchalert.com. Accessed April 12, 2022.

180 ... a *New York Times* story about a banker from Connecticut ...
Michael Wilson, "Did a Banker Kill a Handyman at a Caribbean Resort?
Or Was It Cocaine?" *New York Times*, October 1, 2019, https://www
.nytimes.com/2019/10/01/nyregion/gavin-hapgood-kenny-mitchel
-anguilla-resort.html. Accessed April 12, 2022.

Chapter 10: Death Spiral

194 "... the victim was one of our own ..."
Katie Mettler and Peter Hermann, "Maryland Attorney Found Dead in
His Home After Police Responded to Possible Burglary," *Washington
Post*, February 2, 2021, https://www.washingtonpost.com/local/
public-safety/laurel-homicide-brian-bregman/2021/02/04/a8938d7e
-670e-11eb-8c64-9595888caa15_story.html. Accessed April 13, 2022.
Jackie Bensen, "Slain Laurel Attorney Invited One of the Suspects into
His Home: Police," News4 NBC Washington, February 12, 2021,
https://www.nbcwashington.com/news/local/prince-georges-county/
slain-laurel-attorney-invited-one-of-the-suspects-into-his-home
/2572815/. Accessed April 13, 2022.
Jonathan Franklin, "Police: 3 Additional Suspects Arrested for Murder of
MPD Reserve Officer in Laurel," USA9, March 16, 2021, https://www
.wusa9.com/article/news/crime/mpd-reserve-officer-murdered-3
-arrests-laurel/65-cce7e913-8c2a-48df-8bc5-e6579cc121b6. Accessed
April 13, 2022.

195 Fowler was a member of the Forensic Panel ...
Forensic Panel, https://www.forensicpanel.com. Accessed April 13, 2022.

195 On the witness stand at Chauvin's trial ...
Marie Fazio, "David Fowler, Former Chief Medical Examiner of
Maryland, Says He Believes George Floyd Died from Cardiac
Arrhythmia," *New York Times*, April 14, 2021, https://www.nytimes
.com/2021/04/14/us/david-fowler-maryland-chief-medical-examiner
-testimony.html. Accessed April 13, 2022.

196 Dr. Roger Mitchell ... posted a letter online ...
Letter to Maryland Attorney General Brian Frosh and others, April 20,
2021, https://www.scribd.com/document/507923747/Mitchell-Letter
-re-Fowler-Exhibit-505122021. Accessed April 13, 2022.

**196 Mitchell reportedly had a particular interest in the George Floyd
investigation ...**
Chao Xiong, "Attorneys for Former Officer Charged in George Floyd's
Death Call Medical Examiner's Testimony into Question," *Minneapolis*

Star Tribune, May 12, 2021, https://www.startribune.com/attorneys
-for-former-officer-charged-in-george-floyd-s-death-call-me-s-test
imony-into-question/600056585/. Accessed April 13, 2022.

197 **Three days after Mitchell's letter was posted online . . .**
Rachel Treisman, "Maryland to Probe Cases Handled by Ex-Medical
Examiner Who Testified in Chauvin Trial," NPR, April 24, 2021,
https://www.npr.org/2021/04/24/990536193/maryland-to-probe
-cases-handled-by-ex-medical-examiner-who-testified-in-chauvin-.
Accessed April 13, 2022.

197 **When a *Baltimore Sun* reporter called Fowler . . .**
Phillip Jackson and Justin Fenton, "In-Custody Death Reports Under
Former Maryland Medical Examiner to Be Reviewed After He Testified
Chauvin Did Not Kill George Floyd," *Baltimore Sun*, April 23, 2021,
https://www.baltimoresun.com/news/crime/bs-md-ag-office-review
-20210423-l2oamj3ixnhwznd4545f7pjcau-story.html. Accessed April 13,
2022.

197 **By the time a *Washington Post* reporter reached Fowler . . .**
Emily Davies and Ovetta Wiggins, "Maryland Officials to Launch Review
of Cases Handled by Ex-Chief Medical Examiner Who Testified in
Chauvin's Defense," *Washington Post*, April 23, 2021, https://www
.washingtonpost.com/local/public-safety/maryland-medical-examiner
-investigation-chavin-testimony/2021/04/23/61951580-a2ed-11eb-85fc
-06664ff4489d_story.html. Accessed April 13, 2022.

197 **Nobody batted an eye when Dr. Jonathan Arden . . .**
David Collins, "Goodson Defense Calls Doctor to Refute Medical
Examiner's Findings," WBAL News, November 3, 2017, https://www
.wbaltv.com/article/goodson-defense-calls-doctor-to-refute-medical
-examiners-findings/13149663. Accessed April 13, 2022.
Kevin Rector, "Goodson's Defense Calls Medical Expert as Disciplinary
Trial in Freddie Gray's Case Nears End," *Baltimore Sun*, November 3,
2017, https://www.baltimoresun.com/news/crime/bs-md-goodson
-day-5-story.html. Accessed April 13, 2022.

Epilogue

211 **Jayne Miller, investigative reporter for WBAL News . . .**
Jayne Miller, "I-Team: Backlog of Bodies Await Examination by
Maryland Medical Examiner," WBAL-TV News, January 18, 2022,
https://www.wbaltv.com/article/maryland-medical-examiner
-backlog/38795638. Accessed April 17, 2022.

213 A recent report to Congress . . .

National Institute of Justice, "Needs Assessment of Forensic Laboratories and Medical Examiner/Coroner Offices," Report to Congress, 2006, https://www.justice.gov/olp/page/file/1228306/download. Accessed April 17, 2022.

214 . . . coroners aren't required to have any medical or legal training . . .

Coroner/Medical Examiner Laws, by State, Centers for Disease Control and Prevention, January 15, 2015, https://www.cdc.gov/phlp/publications/topic/coroner.html. Accessed April 2, 2022.

214 Many medical examiner offices lack essential facilities . . .

Randy Hanzlick, "An Overview of Medical Examiner/Coroner Systems in the United States," PowerPoint presentation prepared for National Academies: Forensic Science Needs Committee, undated, https://www.justice.gov/olp/page/file/1228306/download. Accessed April 17, 2022.

214 Scandals and crises have plagued coroner and medical examiner offices . . .

Arthur Kane, "Former Coroner Claimed Iffy Degrees, Did Outside Work on Taxpayer Time," *Las Vegas Review-Journal*, October 20, 2021, https://www.reviewjournal.com/investigations/former-coroner-claimed-iffy-degrees-did-outside-work-on-taxpayer-time-2463081/. Accessed April 2, 2022.

"Two Former Mortuary Technicians of New York Office of Chief Medical Examiner Charged with Stealing Decedents' Property," US Department of Justice, March 30, 2021, https://www.justice.gov/usao-edny/pr/two-former-mortuary-technicians-new-york-city-office-chief-medical-examiner-charged. Accessed April 2, 2022.

Karen Drew, "Defenders Investigations Reveal Mistakes in the Wayne County Morgue: When Is Enough Enough?" WDIV Click on Detroit, February 3, 2022, https://www.clickondetroit.com/news/defenders/2022/02/03/defenders-investigations-reveal-mistakes-in-the-wayne-county-morgue-when-is-enough-enough/. Accessed April 2, 2022.

214 Autopsy backlogs have been reported recently . . .

JoAnn Snoderly, "West Virginia Office of the Chief Medical Examiner Faces Backlog of Cases, Accumulation of Unidentified and Unclaimed Remains," *State Journal*, December 19, 2021, https://www.wvnews.com/statejournal/news/west-virginia-office-of-the-chief-medical-examiner-faces-backlog-of-cases-accumulation-of-unidentified/article_f2bd1c46-4640-11ec-8668-83c3e63c2fbc.html. Accessed March 31, 2021.

Taylor Vance and William Moore, "Delayed After Death: Slow Autopsies at Mississippi Crime Lab Continue to Cause Delays in Court Cases, Funerals," *Daily Journal*, October 4, 2021, https://www.djournal.com/news/state-news/slow-autopsies-at-mississippi-crime-lab-continue-to-cause-delays-in-court-cases-funerals/article_b873e228-33a6-583f-a1b1-707f9c842304.html. Accessed March 31, 2021.

Rachel Swan, "'Explosion of People Dying' Has Led to Huge Backlog of Bodies at the Alameda County Coroner's Office," *San Francisco Chronicle*, February 8, 2022, https://www.sfchronicle.com/eastbay/article/Explosion-of-people-dying-has-led-to-huge-16842677.php. Accessed April 2, 2022.

Joe Ripley, "Reported Backlog at Fulton County Medical Examiner's Office Brings Practices into Question," 11Alive, January 25, 2022, https://www.11alive.com/article/news/local/fulton-county-medical-examiners-office-backlog-practices/85-22ac3457-b87f-42f7-a3b5-9c709b34863d. Accessed April 2, 2022.

Aedan Hannon, "Deaths on the Rise in Southwest Colorado, Putting Stress on County Coroners," *Durango Herald*, March 6, 2022, https://www.durangoherald.com/articles/deaths-on-the-rise-in-southwest-colorado-putting-stress-on-county-coroners/. Accessed April 2, 2022.

214 The Boston medical examiner office . . .

Matt Stout, "State Medical Examiners Cut Autopsy Rates to Among Lowest in Nation," *Boston Globe*, March 6, 2022, https://www.bostonglobe.com/2022/03/06/metro/state-medical-examiners-cut-autopsy-rates-among-lowest-nation/. Accessed April 2, 2022.

215 "We've all seen cases . . ."

Stout, "State Medical Examiners Cut Autopsy Rates."